SIMPLY SUPER
STORYTIMES

Programming Ideas for Ages 3–6

Marie Castellano

UpstartBooks

Fort Atkinson, Wisconsin

For Jasmine and Joshua—
Thank you for putting up with your nutty mother all these years.

Published by UpstartBooks
W5527 Highway 106
P.O. Box 800
Fort Atkinson, Wisconsin 53538-0800
1-800-448-4887

© Marie Castellano, 2003
Cover design: Debra Neu Sletten

The paper used in this publication meets the minimum requirements of American National Standard for Information Science — Permanence of Paper for Printed Library Material. ANSI/NISO Z39.48-1992.

Note: All efforts have been made to obtain permission for the fingerplays and songs in this book. If the author is not listed, the original author is unknown. We apologize for any omissions.

Contents

Introduction 5

Promoting Storytimes 6

Planning a Storytime Program 7

Additional Storytime Resources 9

Snuggle Up Stories 11

Hats Off to Great Books 18

Feel Better Stories 27

Fall Fun 35

Wiggly Good Tales 45

Count on Books 52

Traveling Tales 62

Books, the Greatest Present 70

Cooking Up Good Stories 75

Growing Great Books 81

Flying High Stories 88

Stories Around Town 98

Introduction

Stories can influence paths and change lives. How many of us remember our favorite children's book and how it touched us? Maybe it was because it made us laugh, had a character we could relate to or took us places we always wanted to go. Whatever the reasons, children need to build good memories of books they love. That is why it's important to enhance stories so children remember them. This book helps you plan storytimes with activities that reinforce the stories in children's minds. All of the ideas in this book will build children's confidence and bring them a lifelong love of books.

The crafts and activities in these programs are important learning enhancements. They help parents understand the theme and create an interaction between parent and child. This interaction helps children build comprehension skills and the tangible crafts help reinforce the stories. Seeing the craft helps spark the children's interest in hearing the story again. I suggest listing the storytime books for each theme so parents can read the books with their children and enjoy the experience together. The costumes and props that you use in your storytimes also help enhance children's learning. Anything that is different from their normal routine will draw their attention and bring added interest to learning.

The storytime themes in this book are structured for children ages 3–6. You may wish to vary the themes in order to use them with slightly older children. The book list with each chapter is only a guide and you may wish to add or change the themes according to your needs. Some of the books may be out of print, but they are worthy of mention. I apologize in advance if they are unavailable for purchase, but remember that libraries are a wonderful source for out of print materials.

How to Use This Book

This book is divided into themed storytimes. Each theme begins with the same introductory song. This helps the children know what is going to happen and gets them ready to be a good listener. Once they know the song, it can be fun to do portions fast or slow. Each theme also includes songs, fingerplays and suggested stories to share. Pick and choose which ideas work best for you, then intersperse the fingerplays and songs between the stories. The crafts and activities bring everything together by reinforcing each theme. They can be worked into your storytime wherever you see fit, depending on your available time and the skill level of the children. Theme-appropriate snack ideas are also included. Each storytime ends with the same song. This helps the children recognize when storytime is over.

Promoting Storytimes

The programs in this book are for schools, libraries, bookstores, recreation/park districts, scout troops and anyone else who wants to promote the love of reading to children in a fun way. When planning a program, be sure to consider the age of the child and convenience for the parents. You might consider holding the program more than one time, offering an evening or weekend option or scheduling it when the children are out of school.

Getting the word out depends on your organization. Some ideas include:

- Posters to distribute to local businesses, such as Laundromats and grocery stores. Make sure the poster contains who, what, when, where and why.

- Attach reminder slips to the posters so parents can post them at home.

- If you have a Web site, post all pertinent information on the site. Also post theme-related links to promote extended learning at home.

- Contact the local newspapers and ask to post a community notice. Notifying your local newspaper of a community event might interest them enough to send a photographer and reporter. Or you might ask what section would be appropriate for listing your event. If you do get free publicity, make sure to post it in your scrapbook of events.

- Display a scrapbook that highlights all of the other special events you have done. This should contain pictures taken during your special day and any comments made by parents and participants. Any applicable promotional posters, newspaper articles, etc., can also be included.

- Display any available props, your poster and related materials available for checkout or sale. Set up your display where it will attract people's attention.

- Talk, talk, talk. Word of mouth is your best form of free advertising.

Planning a Storytime Program

Before Storytime

- Decide on your storytime theme and time frame. Then decide which books, activities, songs and fingerplays you will use.

- Set the date and time and determine the number of children you would like to attend.

- Publicize your event.

- Search for props around your classroom, library, school, home and community. You will be surprised by what people have and what they are willing to lend or give away.

- If you plan on serving a snack, let parents know so they can make you aware of possible allergies.

- Obtain the books you will be reading.

- Copy the fingerplays and cut them out. Glue them to 3" x 5" note cards so they are easier to read during storytime.

- Cut and collect materials for art projects.

- Prepare name tags.

Storytime

- Introduce the theme by asking the children about their name tags. Ask why they think these particular name tags were chosen. "What could our storytime be about?" Discuss the props and how they relate to the stories for the day.

- Sing the storytime song to the tune: "London Bridges."

  We're all here for storytime,
  Storytime, storytime. *(Children slap thighs to the beat.)*
  We're all here for storytime,
  Let's get ready.

  Can you turn your ears up high, *(Turn earlobe upward.)*
  Ears up high, ears up high?
  Can you turn your ears up high
  So you can hear? *(Point to children, then ears.)*

  Can you turn your mouth down low, *(Pretend to button lips.)*
  Mouth down low, mouth down low?
  Can you turn your mouth down low?
  Now let's read! *(Fold hands in lap.)*

- Read the stories you have chosen and intersperse fingerplays and songs between the stories.

- Do any of the activities that fit your theme.

- Lead a discussion with the children. Ask them what their favorite book was and what part they liked best. Depending on how many stories were read, you might have to help them remember. Ask questions that are specific to the stories to reinforce comprehension concepts. A good time to talk to the children is when they are doing their art project.

- Serve the storytime snack.

- Sing the goodbye song to the tune: "Where is Thumbkin?"

Where is thumbkin?
Where is thumbkin?
(Have both hands behind your back; bring one hand out at a time showing only your thumb.)
Here I am!
Here I am!

Did you like our stories?* *(Have one thumb "talk" to the other.)*
Yes, I liked our stories!
Time to go, *(Put one hand behind your back.)*
Hide away. *(Place the other hand behind your back.)*

Where are all of you?
Where are all of you?
Here we are! *(Show one hand.)*
Here we are! *(Show other hand.)*

Can you wave goodbye now? *(Wave hand.)*
Yes, we'll wave goodbye now. *(Wave hand.)*
Bye, bye, bye.
Bye, bye, bye.

***Note:** Add or replace verse with "Did you have a good time? / Yes, I had a good time!"*

Additional Storytime Resources

novelties, toys, giftware, party supplies, incentives

Oriental Trading Company
P.O. Box 2308
Omaha, NE 68103
1-800-875-8480
www.orientaltrading.com

Really Good Stuff
Cinema Center
Botsford, CT 06404
1-800-366-1920
www.reallygoodstuff.com

Rinco
Rhode Island Novelty
19 Industrial Lane
Johnston, RI 02919
1-800-528-5599
Fax: 1-800-448-1775
www.rinovelty.com

Smile Makers
P.O. Box 2543
Spartanburg, SC 29304
1-800-825-8085
Fax: 1-800-825-6358
www.smilemakers.com

U.S. Toy Company/Constructive Playthings
13201 Arrington Road
Grandview, MO 64030
1-800-832-0224
www.ustoy.com

Childcraft Education Corp.
P.O. Box 3239
Lancaster, PA 17604
1-800-631-5652
Fax: 1-888-532-4453
www.childcraft.com

Lakeshore Learning Materials
2965 E. Dominguez St.
Carson, CA 90810
1-800-778-4456
www.lakeshorelearning.com

Early Childhood Direct
P.O. Box 369
Landisville, PA 17538
1-800-784-5717
Fax: 1-800-219-5253
www.123ecd.com

Mr. Anderson's Company
211 North Perkins Boulevard
Burlington, WI 53105
262-767-6555
Fax: 262-767-0425

Stampers

Reading, Writing & Rubber Stamps
5158 West 127th St.
Aslip, IL 60803
1-800-842-9768
www.rwrs.com

Snuggle Up Stories
Grandparents, Families and Quilts

Before Storytime

Ask the children to bring a small snuggly blanket or stuffed toy to help them enjoy "snuggling up" during the stories. The blankets can also be used in a later activity.

Name Tags

Copy the name tag patterns on page 17. Make enough copies so you have one name tag per child. Cut the name tags out and color them if you like. Pin the name tag to the child's shirt or punch a hole in it and string it with yarn for a necklace.

Props

- reading glasses
- shawl
- quilt samplers or various styles of quilts
- pictures of family members (various genders, ethnicities and ages make the pictures more interesting)

Note: Quilting guilds and genealogy groups are great resources for quilts and family pictures.

Storytime

- Introduce the theme by asking the children about their name tags.
- Sing the storytime song on page 7.
- Intersperse stories, fingerplays, songs and activities to fit your theme and time frame.

Snack

Serve cookies and milk.

Discussion Questions

Ask specific questions to reinforce comprehension concepts.

For example:

- "Do you and your grandmother read books together like in the book *In Grandmother's Arms*?"
- "Do you do things that are the same but different like in the book *Cherry Pies and Lullabies*?"
- "There are five people in the story *This Is My Family*, how many are in your family?"

Wrapping It Up

Sing the goodbye song on page 8.

Songs

Let's Go See Our Grandparents

Sung to the tune: "Take Me Out to the Ballgame"

Let's go see our grandparents,
Take us there for a while.
Mommy and Daddy both need a break,
We'll play games and we'll stay up real late!

Oh, we want to thank our grandparents,
For all the things that they do.
So it's time to say you're the best,
And that we love you!

To Grandmother's House

Sung to the tune: "Over the River and Through the Woods"

Over the river and through the woods,
To Grandmother's house we go.
The car knows the way,
To go today,
To Grandmother's house, hoo-ray!

Over the river and through the woods,
To Grandmother's house we go.
To play with the toys,
And make lots of noise,
And give Grandma a hug and kiss!
(Make "kiss" sound.)

Mommy's Special

Sung as an echo song to the tune: "Where is Thumbkin?"

Mommy's special,
Mommy's special,
Yes she is!
Yes she is!

And she really loves me,
And she really loves me,
Yes she does!
Yes she does!

(Repeat, changing to daddy, grandma, grandpa, my family, etc.)

Daddy, Daddy, I Love You

Sung to the tune: "Twinkle, Twinkle, Little Star"

Daddy, Daddy, I love you,
Yes I, yes I, yes I do!

I'm so glad that you are mine,
I love you all the time.

Daddy, Daddy, I love you,
Yes I, yes I, yes I do!

Note: *Can change to "Mommy, Mommy, I Love You."*

I Love Mommy

Sung to the tune: "B-I-N-G-O"

There is someone who I love so,
And Mommy is her name.

M-O-M-M-Y
M-O-M-M-Y
M-O-M-M-Y
And Mommy is her name-o!

I love her so much that I give her,
Kisses and hugs, oh!
Kisses and hugs, oh!
Kisses and hugs, oh!
Kisses and hugs, oh!
I love to kiss and hug her.

Note: *Can change to "I Love Daddy."*

I Love My Mommy

Sung to the tune: "Up on the Housetop"

I love my mommy, yessiree!
She is very go-od to me!
She makes me cookies and yummy treats,
That's my mom and she's real neat.

Oh, oh, oh, who wouldn't know,
Oh, oh, oh, who wouldn't know,
I love my mommy and she loves me,
That's the way it's supposed to be.

With My Family

Sung to the tune: "Muffin Man"

Tell me what you like to do,
Like to do, like to do.
Tell me what you like to do,
With your family.

(Child's name) likes to rake the leaves,
Rake the leaves, rake the leaves.
(Repeat child's name) likes to rake the leaves,
With *his/her* family.

(Continue with other children, using their favorite family activity.)

We're a Happy Family

Sung to the tune: "I'm a Little Teapot"

I love Mommy, she loves me,
We love Daddy, yessiree.
He loves us and so you see,
We're a happy family.

(Repeat using brother, sister, grandma, etc.)

Families

Sung to the tune: "Ten Little Indians"

Some have fathers,
Some have mothers,
Some have sisters,
Some have brothers.
In some houses,
There are others.
Every family's special!

Thank You

Sung to the tune: "If You're Happy and You Know It"

When my grandpa gives me something,
I say "thank you."

When my grandma gives me something,
I say "thank you."

I can see it makes them happy,
When I say it so politely.

Yes, good manners mean to always,
Say "thank you!"

Do It For Grandma

Sung to the tune: "Did You Ever See a Lassie?"
Do appropriate actions as you sing.

Let's clap our hands for Grandma,
For Grandma, for Grandma.
Let's clap our hands for Grandma.
Let's clap them this way.
Clap this way and that way,
Clap this way and that way,
Let's clap our hands for Grandma.
Let's clap them this way.

Note: *Add other verses changing Grandma to Grandpa and adding various activities such as read a book with…, dig for worms with Grandpa…, bake cookies with Grandma…, hug ourselves like Grandma would…, etc.*

Let's Make a Quilt

Sung to the tune: "Row, Row, Row Your Boat"

We take a patch from this old shirt,
We take a patch from pants,
We cut more squares and lay them down,
Sew them all together!
Now we have a nice warm quilt,
We sewed it all together!
Now we'll be all warm and snug,
Cuddled in our quilt!

Fingerplays

Grandma's Glasses

Here are Grandma's glasses,
(Fingers form two circles, place in front of eyes.)
And here is Grandma's hat.
(Hands form a hat above head.)
And this is the way she folds her hands,
(Fold hands.)
And puts them in her lap.
(Place hands in lap.)

Note: *Can also change to Grandpa, Mom, Dad, sister, etc. Change voices and actions appropriately.*

Grandma and Grandpa

I love to go to Grandma's house!
(Place hands near heart.)
It's a special place for me.
(Point to self.)
I love to go to Grandma's house.
(Place hands near heart.)
Although I'm only three.
(Hold up three fingers.)

Grandma bakes and Grandma cooks.
(Pretend to stir in a bowl.)
Grandpa does tricks and reads me books.
(Hold hands out as if a book is open.)
Grandma gives me hugs and kisses.
(Hug self, pretend to kiss.)
Grandpa lets me bounce a ball.
(Pretend to bounce a ball.)
They seem to know the special things.
(Place hands near heart.)

That I like best of all!
(Raise both hands out wide.)

Some Families

Some families are large,
(Spread arms out wide.)
Some families are small,
(Bring arms close together.)
But I love my family,
(Cross arms over chest.)
Best of all!

Three in a Family

Here is Daddy, *(Hold up thumb.)*
Here is Mommy, *(Hold up index finger.)*
Here I am for three. *(Hold up pinky.)*
Together we're a family,
As happy as can be! *(Clap!)*

This is My Family

This is my mother, kind and dear.
(Make a fist and point to your thumb.)
This is the father sitting near.
(Show each finger in turn.)
This is the brother strong and tall.
This is the sister, who plays with her ball.
This is the baby, littlest of all.
See my whole family large and small.
(Wiggle all the fingers.)

Mothers are Special

Mothers are special.
They need a hug from you.
They take the time to let us know,
That we are special, too.

Note: *Can change to "Fathers are Special."*

Activities

Paper Quilts

Read *The Keeping Quilt* by Patricia Polacco or *Quilt of Dreams* by Mindy Dwyer. Sing "Let's Make a Quilt," then help the children make paper quilts.

Supplies needed:

- construction paper
- sharpened pencil
- crayons
- markers
- yarn
- tape
- material scraps *(optional)*

Directions:

1. Draw grid-like squares on sheets of construction paper. Cut each piece in half. Give each child a half sheet.

2. Have the children use crayons, markers and material scraps to create designs on the squares.

3. Use a pencil tip to punch two small holes next to each other in two or four places around the sheet. This is so the children can tie their quilt off.

4. Cut short pieces of yarn and tape one end of each piece. Let the children feed the taped end of the yarn down through one hole and up through the other. Tie the yarn pieces into a bow.

5. Repeat in all the sets of holes.

Have books available to show the children various quilt designs. You might also talk about how clothing scraps were sometimes used for quilts. The scraps often tell the story of a family—pants from someone who grew too big, pieces from daddy's childhood blanket, etc.

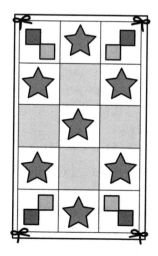

Gross Motor Skills Activity

This is a good lesson in cooperation and listening skills.

1. Have the children place their stuffed toys or blankets in the middle of a quilt.

2. The children should stand around the quilt and grab hold of the edges.

3. Use positional language (e.g., up, down, slow, fast, etc.) to ask the children to move their arms at the same time. Tell the children you would like to see how long they can keep the items on the blanket as it moves. Teamwork helps the movement flow smoothly.

Circle Time Game

1. Place objects such as eyeglasses, a baseball, cookie cutter, kitchen tool, crochet hook, yarn, etc., on a tray.

2. Ask the children to name the items and their uses. If they are not familiar with an item they should describe it.

3. Discuss who in a family would use each item.

4. Cover the tray with a cloth. Discreetly remove one item and keep it hidden in the cloth. Ask the children to tell you what is missing. Repeat with other items.

Note: Use the age of the children as a guide for the number of items on your tray.

Math Activity

Make number cards out of various colors of construction paper squares. Place them in a quilt pattern. Have the children place the correct number of play people on each number card. Then have them find the number that matches the amount of people in their family.

Fine Motor Skills Activity

Have the children use shoelaces and large buttons to practice sewing. If you cannot find real buttons with large holes, cut circles from thin cardboard and punch holes in them to make your own buttons. This is a good time to teach basic concepts such as "in and out"

and "up and down." This also helps occupy a child until a caregiver arrives.

Storytime Books to Share

Books About Grandparents

Apple Juice Tea by Martha Weston. Houghton Mifflin, 1994. When Gran comes to visit, Polly wishes she would go home, until one night when Gran baby-sits.

Bluebird Summer by Deborah Hopkinson. HarperCollins, 2001. Two children create a living memorial for their grandmother who loved gardens and bluebirds.

Grandfather's Journey by Allen Say. Houghton Mifflin, 1993. A Japanese American man recounts his grandfather's journey to America. He undertakes the journey and experiences the feelings of being torn by a love for two different countries.

Grandma According to Me by Karen Magnuson Beil. Dell Publishing Co., 1994. A girl lovingly tells a story of how she sees her grandma.

Grandma is Somebody Special by Susan Goldman Rubin. A. Whitman, 1987. A child enjoys visiting her grandmother in a tall apartment building in a big city.

Grandmas Are for Giving Tickles by Harriet Ziefert. Penguin Putnam, 2000. A grandma will take you on new adventures and play dress-up. Grandmas explain the rules and give you tickles. And grandmas love to hug you!

Grandmother Winter by Phyllis Root. Houghton Mifflin, 1999. When Grandmother Winter shakes out her feather quilt, birds, bats, bears and other creatures prepare themselves for the cold.

Grandpa and Me Together by Susan Goldman. A. Whitman, 1980. Katherine spends the day doing special things with her grandfather.

Grandpas are for Finding Worms by Harriet Ziefert. Penguin Putnam, 2000. It's fun to spend time with Grandpa. He helps you find wiggly worms for fishing and holds hands when you go out. A grandpa always makes you feel special.

In Grandmother's Arms by Jayne C. Shelton. Scholastic, 2001. A young girl is able to go anywhere her imagination takes her when she reads with her grandmother in their Storybook Chair.

In the Morning Mist by Eleanor J. Lapp. A. Whitman, 1978. A young child and a grandfather set out on a fishing expedition and find the countryside transformed by the morning fog.

The Moon Came Too by Nancy White Carlstrom. Simon & Schuster, 1987. A young child excitedly plans all the essentials she must take on a trip to Grandma's house.

No Kiss for Grandpa by Harriet Ziefert. Scholastic, 2001. After he and his grandfather spend the day doing what Louie wants to do, the young kitten gives Grandpa the best kiss ever.

No Mirrors in my Nana's House by Ysaye M. Barnwell. Harcourt, 1998. A girl discovers her beauty by looking into her Nana's eyes.

Our Granny by Margaret Wild. Houghton Mifflin, 1998. Two young children present a catalog of all the varying sizes, shapes and types of grandmothers, interspersed with loving comments about their own granny.

Spot Visits His Grandparents by Eric Hill. Penguin Putnam, 1999. Spot the dog spends the day with his grandparents.

When Grandma Came by Jill Paton Walsh. Penguin Putnam, 1994. Madeline's grandmother has roamed the wide world over, but always returns to her beloved young granddaughter to assure her that she is the greatest wonder of all.

When I Am Old With You by Angela Johnson. Orchard Books, 1993. A child imagines being old with Grandaddy and enjoying their favorite activities.

Zero Grandparents by Michelle Edwards. Harcourt, 2001. Calliope does not have a grandmother or grandfather to bring to school on Grandparent's Day, but she finds a special way to participate anyway.

Books About Families

Cherry Pies and Lullabies by Lynn Reiser. Greenwillow Books, 1998. Four generations of mothers and daughters express their love through family traditions that are the same but different.

Daddies Are for Catching Fireflies by Harriet Ziefert. Penguin Putnam, 1999. A daddy tries to fix your toys, answer your questions and always has the best seat at the parade.

Dancing the Breeze by George Shannon. Bradbury Press, 1991. Lyrically describes Papa, a young daughter and the evening breeze as they dance among the flowers in the front yard while the moon rises.

Just Me and My Dad by Mercer Mayer. Golden Press, 1977. Father and son go on a camping trip.

Just Me and My Mom by Mercer Mayer. Western Pub. Co., 1990. Little Critter and his mother take a trip to the city.

Mine! by Kevin Luthardt. Atheneum Books for Young Readers, 2001. Two brothers fight over the new toy their grandmother sent them until it breaks and they learn to share.

Mommies Are for Counting Stars by Harriet Ziefert. Penguin USA, 1999. A mommy is wonderful in so many ways. She knows how to kiss a boo-boo and make it better, give baths and all kinds of extra-special things.

The Relatives Came by Cynthia Rylant. Aladdin Books, 1993. The relatives come to visit from Virginia and everyone has a wonderful time.

This Is My Family by Gina Mayer. Random House, 1992. Little Critter introduces his family.

What Dads Can't Do by Douglas Wood. Simon & Schuster Books for Young Readers, 2000. Describes how dads show love by explaining all the things that they cannot do, such as sleeping late, keeping their ties clean and reading books by themselves.

What Moms Can't Do by Douglas Wood. Simon & Schuster Books for Young Readers, 2001. A child ponders the many problems that mothers must deal with in the course of a normal day.

Books About Quilts

The Keeping Quilt by Patricia Polacco. Simon & Schuster Books for Young Readers, 1998. A home-made quilt ties together the lives of four generations of an immigrant Jewish family, remaining a symbol of their enduring love and faith.

The Log Cabin Quilt by Ellen Howard. Holiday House, 1997. When Elvirey and her family move to a log cabin in the Michigan woods, something even more important than Granny's quilt pieces makes the new dwelling a home.

Luka's Quilt by Georgia Guback. HarperCollins, 1994. When Luka's grandmother makes a traditional Hawaiian quilt for her, she and Luka disagree over the colors it should include.

The Name Quilt by Phyllis Root. Farrar, Straus and Giroux, 2003. One of Sadie's favorite things to do when she visits her grandmother is to hear stories about the family members whose names are on a special quilt that Grandma handmade, so Sadie is very sad when the quilt is blown away in a storm.

Quilt of Dreams by Mindy Dwyer. Graphic Arts Center Publishing Co., 2000. While working on a quilt that her grandmother started before she died, Katy discovers the special memories and meanings that are part of every quilt.

Name Tag Patterns for Snuggle Up Stories

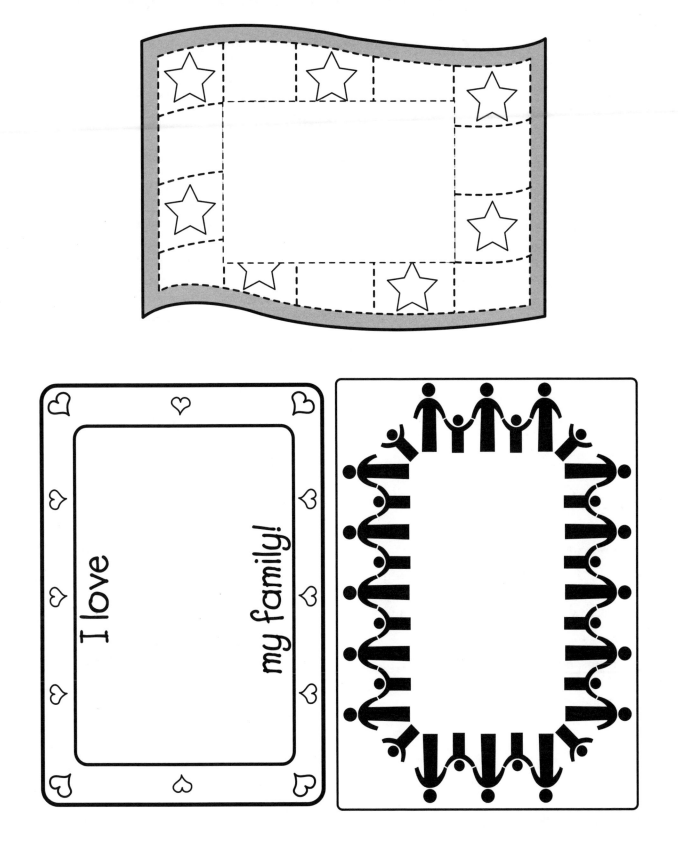

I love
my family!

Hats Off to Great Books

Hats, Clothing and Dressing Order

Before Storytime

Name Tags

Copy the name tag patterns on pages 25–26. Make enough copies so you have one name tag per child. Cut the name tags out and color them if you like. Pin the name tag to the child's shirt or punch a hole in it and string it with yarn for a necklace.

Props

- Hats—wear as many hats piled on your head as you can. Or create a hat with plastic flowers, party streamers, ribbons, etc., coming out of it. Wear anything that will attract attention.

Storytime

- Introduce the theme by asking the children about their name tags.
- Ask, "Do you like my hat(s)?" "Do you have a hat?" "When do you wear hats?" "Have you ever worn a hat just for fun?"
- Sing the storytime song on page 7.
- Intersperse stories, fingerplays, songs and activities to fit your theme and time frame.

Snack

Serve cupcakes with the paper cup folded down to make a hat with a brim.

Discussion Questions

Ask specific questions to reinforce comprehension concepts.

For example:

- "In *Froggy Gets Dressed,* what did Froggy learn when he tried to get dressed to go outside?" (A fun way to demonstrate this is to put on very bulky gloves and then try to tie your shoes, put on big boots or even button your coat. Get silly and try to put a shirt on over your coat or socks on over your boots. This allows the children to see the dressing order concept in a fun way.)

Wrapping It Up

Sing the goodbye song on page 8.

Songs

Dressing in the Morning

Sung to the tune: "This is the Way"

This is the way we get dressed in the morning,
Dressed in the morning,
Dressed in the morning.
This is the way we get dressed in the morning,
So early in the day!

This is the way we put on our shirt,
Put on our shirt,
Put on our shirt,
This is the way we put on our shirt,
So early in the morning!

(Act out each movement and continue adding items of clothing depending on the season: socks, shoes, snow pants, raincoat, etc.)

What Are You Wearing?

Sung to the tune: "Johnny Pounds"

(Child's name) wears a red shirt,
Red shirt, red shirt.
(Child's name) wears a red shirt today!

Note: *Can be used as a good introduction to the beginning of the program. Name each child and a different color and piece of clothing they are wearing. You may also add:*

Did anyone wear mittens, mittens, mittens,
Did anyone wear mittens today?

Additional lines could use coat, scarf, boots, etc.

What Do I Wear?

Sung to the tune: "For He's a Jolly Good Fellow"

What do I wear on my feet?
What do I wear on my feet?
What do I wear on my feet
That you have to tie or buckle? *(shoes)*

What do I put over my legs?
What do I put over my legs?
What do I put over my legs
That need to be zipped up? *(pants)*

What do I wear on my head?
What do I wear on my head?
What do I wear on my head
To keep me warm outside?
(To keep the sun off me?) *(a hat)*

What goes over my shirt?
What goes over my shirt?
What goes over my shirt
When I go outside to play? *(a jacket)*

Proper Order

Sung to the tune: "Here we go Round the Mulberry Bush"

First my socks go on my feet,
Then my feet go in my shoes.
If I did it the other way,
It wouldn't be so neat!

Dressing

Sung to the tune: "Johnny Pounds"

Children put your pants on,
Pants on, pants on.
Children put your pants on,
One, two, three.

Children put your socks on …

Children put your shoes on …

Children put your shirt on …

Children put your sweater on …

(Continue with other pieces of clothing. Mix it up and be silly saying shoes then socks, etc. See if the children catch the mix-up. If not, ask why that would be silly. Could I put my shoes and then my socks on?)

Getting Dressed

Sung to the tune: "The Farmer in the Dell"
Do appropriate actions as you sing.

I'm getting dressed myself,
I'm getting dressed myself.
Hi-ho, I'm growing up,
I'm getting dressed myself.

I'm putting on my shirt.
I'm putting on my shirt.
Hi-ho, I'm growing up,
I'm putting on my shirt.

I'm putting on my pants.
I'm putting on my undies.
I'm putting on my socks.
I'm putting on my shoes.

Now look what I have done.
Now look what I have done.
Hi-ho, I'm growing up,
Now see what I can do!

Winter Dress Song

Sung to the tune: "London Bridges"
Do appropriate actions as you sing.

Winter winds are blowing hard,
Blowing hard, blowing hard.
Winter winds are blowing hard,
What shall we wear?

Put on mittens and a scarf,
And a coat, with a hat.
Button up and bundle tight,
That's what you wear!

Additional Suggestions

Head, Shoulders, Knees and Toes
Traditional

Head, shoulders, knees and toes,
Knees and toes.

Head, shoulders, knees and toes,
Knees and toes.

And eyes, and ears, and mouth,
And nose.

Head, shoulders, knees and toes,
Knees and toes.

One, Two, Buckle My Shoe *Traditional*

One, two,
Buckle my shoe.

Three, four,
Shut the door.

Five, six,
Pick up sticks.

Seven, eight,
Lay them straight.

Nine, ten,
Do it again!

Fingerplay

Grandma's Glasses

Variation of Traditional

Here are Grandma's glasses,
And here is Grandma's hat.
And this is the way she folds her hands,
And puts them in her lap.

Here are Grandpa's glasses,
(Make your voice a bit louder and deeper.)
And here is Grandpa's hat.
And this is the way he folds his hands,
And puts them in his lap.

Note: I cross my arms over my chest for Grandpa, that way you can tell the children you'll know if

they are sitting like Grandma or Grandpa just by the way they fold their hands to listen.

Activities

Paper Doll Clothes

Read *Crazy Clothes* by Niki Yektai or *Froggy Gets Dressed* by Jonathan London. Then have the children make clothes for a paper doll.

Supplies needed:

*   scissors
*   material scraps cut in clothing shapes (see page 24)
*   glue
*   crayons or markers
*   yarn

Directions:

1. Use the patterns on page 23 and have the children choose a paper doll to dress.

2. Have the children use the material scraps to glue clothes onto the boy or girl.

3. They can use the crayons or markers to add features and the yarn to add hair.

Hat

Read *Caps For Sale: A Tale of a Peddler, Some Monkeys, and their Monkey Business* by Esphyr Slobodkina or *Who Took the Farmer's Hat?* by Joan L. Nodset. Then have the children make their own hat.

Supplies needed:

*   large Styrofoam plate (one for each child)
*   Styrofoam bowl (one for each child)
*   glue
*   tissue paper
*   tape or stapler
*   construction paper
*   silk flowers, curling ribbon, sequins, glitter, ribbon, streamers, etc.
*   markers

Directions:

1. Turn the plate upside down and glue the upside-down bowl to the plate.

2. Cover the hat with a sheet of tissue paper. Staple, glue or tape the tissue paper to the plate.

3. Have the children add decorations to personalize the hat.

Gross Motor Skills Activity

Use a flat hat or one that easily collapses to play this circle game.

Directions:

1. Choose one child to be It and have all of the other children sit in a circle.

2. Have the child who is It sit in the center of the circle and cover his or her eyes.

3. Have one child hide the hat behind his or her back. The rest of the children should put their hands behind their backs and pretend to have the hat. Everyone says, "*(Child's name, child's name)* where's my hat? The wind blew it from my head how can I get it back?"

3. The child who is It has one chance to guess who has the hat. If he or she guesses right, the child who had the hat goes in the center and is It. If the child does not guess correctly, the child who had the hat shows it and becomes It.

Science Activity

The clothes we wear in different types of weather is a basic science lesson. Ask questions such as,

- "If I were going to the beach would I wear (put on a scarf and mittens) this?"

- "Why do we wear hats in the winter?"

- "Would a straw hat help keep me warm?"

- "When would I wear a hat like this?"

- "Why would I wear a hat that doesn't keep my head warm?"

Have various pieces of clothes to try on and play with. Ask, "Where might I be going if I wore (hold up or put on various pieces of clothes) this?" Allow the children to try on clothes and tell a short story of where they are going and what they would do there.

Have the children sort the clothes according to seasons.

Math Activity

Read *The Mitten: A Ukrainian Folktale* adapted by Jan Brett.

Have two pieces of felt cut into mitten shapes. Use Velcro to keep the sides together. Fill them with plastic animals. Have the children count how many fit inside the mitten until it bursts.

Fine Motor Skills Activity

Cut out pictures of hats from catalogs. Have the children match the hats according to the color or season they are worn in. Match any hats that are the same.

Storytime Books to Share

Bird's New Shoes by Chris Riddell. Henry Holt & Co., 1987. Rat, Goat, Snake and other animals get into a frenzy over the latest fashion in clothing.

Caps for Sale: A Tale of a Peddler, Some Monkeys, and their Monkey Business by Esphyr Slobodkina. HarperCollins, 1987. Monkeys steal the peddler's caps and mimic his actions.

The Cat and the Bird in the Hat by Norman Bridwell. Scholastic, 2000. After quarreling over ownership of a hat, the cat and bird find that by sharing it they create a wonderful friendship.

Crazy Clothes by Niki Yektai. Simon & Schuster, 1994. When Patrick tries to show he can dress himself, the clothes become contrary and insist on going on the wrong parts of his body.

The 500 Hats of Bartholomew Cubbins by Dr. Seuss. Random House, 1989. Each time Bartholomew Cubbins attempts to obey the King's order to take off his hat, he finds there is another one on his head.

Froggy Gets Dressed by Jonathan London. Penguin Putnam, 1994. Rambunctious Froggy hops out into the snow for a winter frolic, but is called back by his mother to put on some necessary articles of clothing.

The Hat by Jan Brett. Putnam, 1997. A hedgehog amuses other animals with his explanations of why the stocking is stuck on his head.

Hats, Hats, Hats by Ann Morris. William Morrow & Co., 1993. Photos of hats from different countries. Index in back briefly explains hats.

Hello Cat, You Need a Hat by Rita Golden Gelman. Scholastic, 1999. A mouse tries to convince a grumpy cat to wear a variety of hats.

How the Trollusk Got His Hat by Mercer Mayer. Western Pub. Co., 1979. When stamp-collecting Trollusk returns Reggie McLeod's new squeezle skin hat, they become friends.

I Hate Boots! by Harriet Ziefert. HarperCollins, 1991. A child gives her mother a hard time about getting dressed for winter to go outside.

Miss Fannie's Hat by Jan Karon. Penguin Putnam, 2001. When ninety-nine-year-old Miss Fannie gives up her favorite pink straw hat with the roses to help raise money for her church, she receives an unexpected reward.

The Missing Mitten Mystery by Steven Kellogg. Penguin Putnam, 2002. Annie searches the whole neighborhood for her mitten, the fifth she's lost that winter.

The Mitten: A Ukrainian Folktale adapted by Jan Brett. Putnam, 1989. Several animals sleep snugly in Nicki's lost mitten until the bear sneezes.

New Blue Shoes by Eve Rice. Penguin Putnam, 1978. A girl goes shopping with her mother for new shoes which, she insists, must be blue.

Shoes by Elizabeth Winthrop. Harper Collins, 1988. A survey of the many kinds of shoes in the world concludes that the best of all are the perfect natural shoes that are your feet.

Underwear! by Mary Elise Monsell. A. Whitman, 1993. Bismark the Buffalo is grumpy and unlovable until his friends teach him how to laugh and show him that wearing colorful underwear can be great fun.

What Can You Do With a Shoe? by Beatrice Schenk de Regniers. Simon & Schuster, 1997. What can you do with a shoe? You can put it on your ear or wear it on your head or butter it like bread. A delightful rhyming story with a sense of play.

Whose Hat? by Margaret Miller. Econo-Clad Books, 1999. Children are shown wearing hats that represent various occupations.

Who Took the Farmer's Hat? by Joan L. Nodset. HarperCollins, 1988. The wind blows the farmer's hat away and he finds it being used in a most surprising way.

Paper Doll Patterns

Paper Doll Clothing Patterns

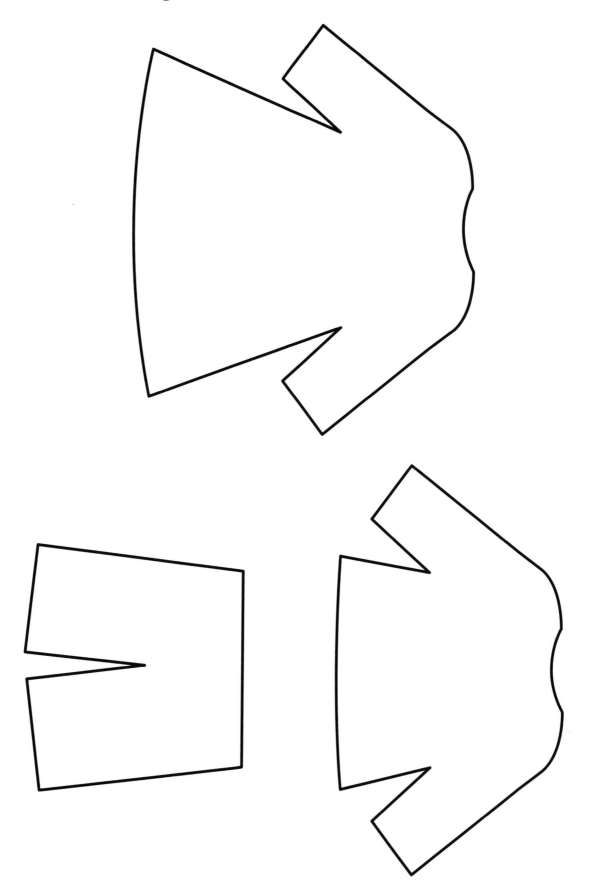

Name Tag Patterns for Hats Off to Great Books

Name Tag Patterns for Hats Off to Great Books

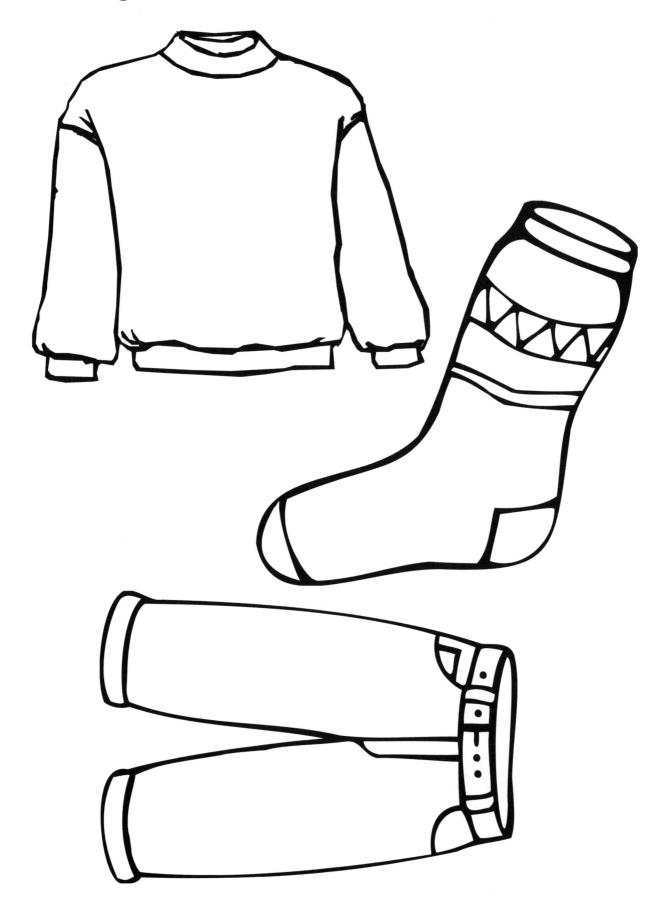

Feel Better Stories

Feelings, Being Sick, Health, Doctors and Hospitals

Before Storytime

Name Tags

Copy the name tag patterns on page 34. Make enough copies so you have one name-tag per child. Cut the name tags out and color them if you like. Pin the name tag to the child's shirt or punch a hole in it and string it with yarn for a necklace.

Props

- Make hearts with various faces (happy, sad, mad, etc.) and Velcro them to yourself. Use a Velcro apron if you have one, otherwise a sweater works well. (For ideas and help with your feelings faces see *www.confidentkids.com*. Click on resource catalog, then other resources to view the "How are you feeling today?" poster.)

- Wear a stethoscope or buy an old lab coat from a resale or second hand shop. Clinics or doctors' offices are often willing to lend props for a short time.

- Carry in a box of tissues and pretend to sneeze. (Be sure to inform parents that this is part of the program.)

Storytime

- Introduce the theme by asking the children about their name tags.

- Ask, "Why am I dressed like this?" "Who do you think I am pretending to be today?" "What are these faces on me about?" "How are you feeling today?" "Have you ever been sad, sick or happy?"

- Sing the storytime song on page 7.

- Intersperse stories, fingerplays, songs and activities to fit your theme and time frame.

Snack

Serve a healthy snack of applesauce, saltine crackers with cheese and orange juice.

Discussion Questions

Ask specific questions to reinforce comprehension concepts.

For example:

- "What did mommy bring to the boy in the book *I Have a Cold?*" "What did daddy give him?"

- "Do you rest, read, eat and play when you are sick like in the book *Itchy, Itchy Chicken Pox?*"

Wrapping It Up

Sing the goodbye song on page 8.

Songs

The Doctor's Song

Sung to the tune: "Row, Row, Row, Your Boat"

I use a stethoscope
To listen to your heart,
To help you be a healthy child,
And heal you when you aren't.

My Doctor

Sung to the tune: "My Bonnie Lies Over the Ocean"

My doctor helps me when I feel bad,
She makes people feel well.
I really do like my doctor,
She helps everyone feel swell.

Doctors, doctors,
They help us feel much better.
Doctors, doctors,
They help us all when we're sick.

I'm a Helpful Doctor

Sung to the tune: "I'm a Little Teapot"

I'm a helpful doctor, dressed in white.
I help people both day and night.
When you get hurt or sick, see me,
I'll get you all fixed up as quick as can be!

Doctors Make Us Well

Sung to the tune: "Farmer in the Dell"

The doctor makes us well.
The doctor makes us well.
Hey! Ho! What do you know?
The doctor makes us well.

To the Hospital

Sung to the tune: "Frére Jacque"
Do as an echo song.

To the hospital.
To the hospital.
We will go.
We will go.
We will see the doctors.
We will see the doctors.
We will see the nurses.
We will see the nurses.
All in white.
All in white.
Here we go.
Here we go.

Wash Your Hands

Sung to the tune: "Row, Row, Row, Your Boat"

Wash, wash, wash your hands,
Play our hand wash game.
Rub and scrub and scrub and rub,
Germs go down the drain, hey!

Wash, wash, wash your hands,
Play our handy game.
Rub and scrub and scrub and rub,
Dirt goes down the drain, hey!

The Wiggle Song

Sung to the tune: "For He's a Jolly Good Fellow"

My thumbs are starting to wiggle,
(Wiggle thumbs.)
My thumbs are starting to wiggle,
My thumbs are starting to wiggle,
Around, around, around.

My hands are starting to wiggle …
(Wiggle hands.)

My arms are starting to wiggle …
(Wiggle arms.)

My toes … *(Wiggle toes.)*

My feet … *(Wiggle feet.)*

My legs … *(Wiggle legs.)*

My head … *(Shake head.)*

All of me is starting to wiggle,
*(Jump up and down while shaking all body
parts.)*
All of me is starting to wiggle,
All of me is starting to wiggle,
And now I need to rest!
(Sit and put your head in your hands as in sleep.)

Put Your Finger in the Air

*Sung to the tune: "If You're Happy and You
Know It"*
Do appropriate actions as you sing.

Put your finger in the air, in the air.
Put your finger in the air, in the air.
Put your finger in the air,
And leave it there about a year.

Put your finger in the air, in the air.

Put your finger on your head …
Tell me is it green or is it red?

Put your finger on your nose …
And let the cold winds blow.
(Make blowing sound.)

Put your finger on your chin …
That's where the food slips in.

Put your finger on your shoe …
Leave it there a day or two.

Put your finger on your cheek …
And leave it there a week.

Put your fingers all together, all together.
Put your fingers all together, all together.
Put your fingers all together,
And we'll clap for better weather.
Put your fingers all together and all clap.

Fingerplays and Poem

Five Senses

Smelling is just so divine,
(Sniff air.)
I do it with my nose so fine.
(Point to nose.)

Hearing is a great delight, *(Cup ears.)*
I use my ears left and right.
(Point to the left then the right.)

Tasting is a special treat,
(Point to mouth.)
I love my tongue on something sweet.
(Lick lips.)

Seeing brings the world in view,
(Focus a telescope with hands.)
See my eyes here, one and two.
(Point to eyes.)

Touching's fun and as easy as can be,
(Wiggle fingers.)
'Cause I can feel with all of me.
(Wiggle whole body.)

Here is My Body

(Point to each part of the body as you say the rhyme.)

Here are my ears and here is my nose.

Here are my fingers and here are my toes.
Here are my eyes, both open wide.
Here is my mouth with my teeth inside.
And my busy tongue that helps me speak.
Here is my chin and here are my cheeks.
Here are my hands that help me to play,
And my feet that run about all day.
(Run in place.)

Myself
by Paula Peck

Sometimes I feel angry,
And sometimes I feel sad.
Sometimes I feel frightened,
And sometimes I feel glad.
But all the time I'm feeling,
I hope you will agree—
I have one feeling that won't change.
I'm happy to be me!

Activities

Achoo! Faces

Read *I Have a Cold* by Grace Maccarone, *I Love to Sneeze* by Ellen Schecter or *Elmo Says, Achoo!* by Sarah Albee. Then make Achoo! faces.

Supplies needed:

- paper plate (one for each child)
- crayons or markers
- yarn
- scissors
- facial tissue (one for four children)
- glue

Directions:

1. Have the children draw a face on the bottom of a paper plate. Add yarn for hair.

2. Use the pattern on the next page to copy one hand for each child. Cut the hands out or have each child cut his or her own. Adjust the length as needed.

3. Cut the facial tissue into fourths, one piece for each child.

Hand Pattern

4. Let the children glue the piece of tissue to the paper hand. Then glue the hand to the face. Make sure the arm is long enough so it can cover the mouth.

Discuss how germs spread and make people sick. Remind the children that covering their mouths is a way to help keep others healthy.

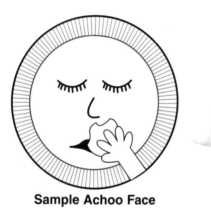

Sample Achoo Face

Open Up and Say "AAAAAH!"

Read *The Good Bad Day* by Charnan Simon or *Felix Feels Better* by Rosemary Wells. Discuss what it's like to go to the doctor. Then make Aaaaah! faces.

Supplies needed:

- flesh colored paper
- scissors
- crayons or markers
- yarn
- tongue depressors (one for each child)

Directions:

1. Copy the face pattern on page 33 onto flesh colored paper. Make one face for each child.

2. Have the children cut the faces out and add eyes and a nose. (You may wish to discuss how faces look when they feel a certain way. Demonstrate or have the children demonstrate various faces.)

3. Let the children add yarn for hair, then color a tongue so it protrudes from the mouth. Pass out tongue depressors.

Get Well Soon Cards

Read *Hiccups, Hiccups* by Rae Bains, *Get Well, Clown-Arounds!* by Joanna Cole or *Itchy, Itchy Chicken Pox* by Grace Maccarone. Then have the children make a get well card for one of the characters in the stories. Discuss how we feel when we are sick or when someone we love is. Ask the children if they have ever gotten a card when they were sick or if they ever made a card to send to someone who was sick.

Supplies needed:

- paper or construction paper
- crayons or markers
- scissors
- old cards for decoration *(optional)*
- glue *(optional)*

Directions:

1. Fold a piece of construction paper in half.

2. Have the children decorate the cards with crayons or markers.

3. If they like, they can cut out pictures from old cards and glue them on.

4. Write a get well message inside the card.

Gross Motor Skills Activity

Read *Freddie Visits the Doctor* by Nicola Smee, *Doctor Maisy* by Lucy Cousins or *My Doctor, My Friend* by P. K. Hallinan. Play the traditional "Head, Shoulders, Knees and Toes" from page 20, varying in speed and order for fun. Then sing "Put Your Fingers in the Air" and "The Wiggle Song" on page 28.

Science Activity

Play a body awareness game. Gather items such as a watch, scarf, shoe, sock, shirt, pants, skirt, ring, barrette, earrings, bracelet, hat, etc. Place all of the items in a bag. Pull out one item at a time and have the children tell you what part of the body it goes on and why.

- Could a pair of pants fit on your arm? Will the sock fit on your head? Discuss the various body parts and what they do.

- Why don't we wear any special clothing over our heart? How does the body cover it for us? Have them feel for their ribs. Explain how our skin and nails protect us.

- Why is it important to cover our feet? Why don't we need to keep them covered all the time? You may want to bring in how the elements affect our bodies.

After you are dressed up have the children count the items you have on (or use a child to demonstrate). How many are in a pair? How many pairs of things are there? How many things does everyone have on today? Have everyone count and see who has on the most items.

Fine Motor Skills Activity

Have the children play hospital with the dolls and teddy bears as the patients. They can use gauze, Ace bandages, Band-Aids and a doctor bag to play doctor or nurse.

Feeling Faces

Draw several faces that are missing the mouth and eyebrows on small paper plates. Use brown, black and yellow construction paper to make eyebrows of varying shapes. Use red and pink construction paper to make mouths showing various feelings (happy, sad, mad, silly, etc.). Have the parts available for the children to create different faces. Discuss the feelings their faces are expressing.

Storytime Books to Share

Books About Being Sick, Health, Doctors and Hospitals

At the Doctor by Christopher Forsey. Franklin Watts, 1983. Shows various things a doctor will do when you go see him. A "Look Back and Find" section provides additional information and asks questions relating to the story.

Doctor Maisy by Lucy Cousins. Candlewick Press, 2001. Maisy and Tallulah play doctor and nurse.

Don't You Feel Well, Sam? by Amy Hest. Candlewick Press, 2002. Mrs. Bear provides just the right TLC for her under-the-weather cub.

Elmo Says, Achoo! by Sarah Albee. Random House, 2000. Elmo's repeated sneezes create havoc on Sesame Street.

Felix Feels Better by Rosemary Wells. Candlewick Press, 2001. Felix feels bad and does not want to eat or play, so his mother takes him to Doctor Duck, who makes everything better.

Freddie Visits the Doctor by Nicola Smee. Little Barron's, 1999. Freddie gets a sore throat and visits the doctor.

Germs Make Me Sick by Melvin Berger. HarperCollins, 1996. Explains how bacteria and viruses affect the human body and how the body fights them.

Get Well, Clown-Arounds! by Joanna Cole. Gareth Stevens Pub., 1993. A wacky family thinks that they have become very sick when they look in the mirror and see green spots.

Going to the Hospital by Fred Rogers. Putnam, 1988. Describes what happens during a stay in the hospital, including some of the common forms of medical treatment.

The Good Bad Day by Charnan Simon. Millbrook Press, 1998. Pam is sick and having a very bad day until her parents and her friends help to cheer her up.

Hiccups, Hiccups by Rae Bains. Troll Associates, 1981. Rosy Rabbit has the hiccups and her friends are sure they can stop them.

Itchy, Itchy Chicken Pox by Grace Maccarone. Scholastic, 1992. Peppy rhymes present the humorous side to a common ailment.

I Have a Cold by Grace Maccarone. Scholastic, 1998. A sick child describes how it feels to have a bad cold.

I Love to Sneeze by Ellen Schecter. Bantam, 1992. A lover of sneezes describes the havoc wrought by such nasal explosions, which have the power to blow the whiskers off the cat and make freckles jump noses.

I Wish I Was Sick, Too! by Franz Brandenberg. Puffin Books, 1978. Elizabeth envies the pampered treatment her brother gets when he is sick in bed, until she gets sick, too.

Madeline by Ludwig Bemelmans. Puffin Books, 1998. Nothing frightens Madeline—not tigers, not mice, not even getting sick. To Madeline, a trip to the hospital is a grand adventure.

Miss Bindergarten Stays Home From Kindergarten by Joseph Slate. Dutton Children's Books, 2000. Miss Bindergarten is struck by the flu on Sunday and knows she'll have to stay home from kindergarten on Monday, but a substitute is ready.

Mother, Mother, I Feel Sick, Send For the Doctor, Quick Quick Quick by Remy Charlip and Burton Supree. Tricycle Press, 2001. When a boy complains of feeling sick, his distressed mother sends for the doctor. The doctor operates on the boy's stomach and extracts one impossible object after another, from a teapot to a bicycle.

My Doctor, My Friend by P. K. Hallinan. Ideals Children's Books, 1996. A visit to the doctor is shown to be nothing to fear.

No Mail for Mitchell by Catherine Siracusa. Random House, 1990. Mitchell delivers mail to his neighbors but does not receive any mail himself. When he comes down with the flu, he finally gets mail, which convinces him he is loved and missed.

Books About Feelings

The Feel Good Book by Todd Parr. Little, Brown, 2002. Inspiring words and pictures about all the special things that make us feel good.

Glad Monster, Sad Monster: A Book About Feelings by Ed Emberley and Anne Miranda. Little, Brown, 1997. Monsters of different colors explain what makes them feel glad, sad, loving, worried, silly and angry. Fold-out masks encourage readers to talk about their feelings.

The Feelings Book by Todd Parr. Little, Brown, 2000. Children express different moods, including "I feel very mad," "I feel like reading books all day" and "I feel like wearing funny underwear."

How I Feel series by Marcia Leonard. Bantam Books. Includes angry, happy, scared and silly. Interactive books to help children understand their feelings.

I Feel Happy, and Sad, and Angry, and Glad by Mary Murphy. Dorling Kindersley Pub., 2000. Canine friends express a wide range of emotions as they play, argue and make up.

My Many Colored Days by Dr. Seuss. Knopf, 1996. Rhyming verse that associates colors with emotions.

Sometimes I Feel Like a Storm Cloud by Lezlie Evans. Mondo, 1999. A child describes how it feels to experience a variety of emotions.

Sometimes I'm a Bombaloo by Rachel Vail. Scholastic, 2002. When Katie Honors feels angry and out of control, her mother helps her to be herself again.

Today I Feel Silly & Other Moods that Make My Day by Jamie Lee Curtis. HarperCollins, 1998. A child's emotions range from silliness to anger to excitement, coloring and changing each day.

What Makes Me Happy? by Catherine and Laurence Anholt. Candlewick Press, 1995. Children describe in rhyming verse their feelings and what makes them feel different ways.

When Sophie Gets Angry—Really, Really Angry by Molly Bang. Blue Sky Press, 1999. A young girl is upset and doesn't know how to manage her anger, but takes the time to cool off and regain her composure.

Patterns for Open Up and Say "AAAAH!"

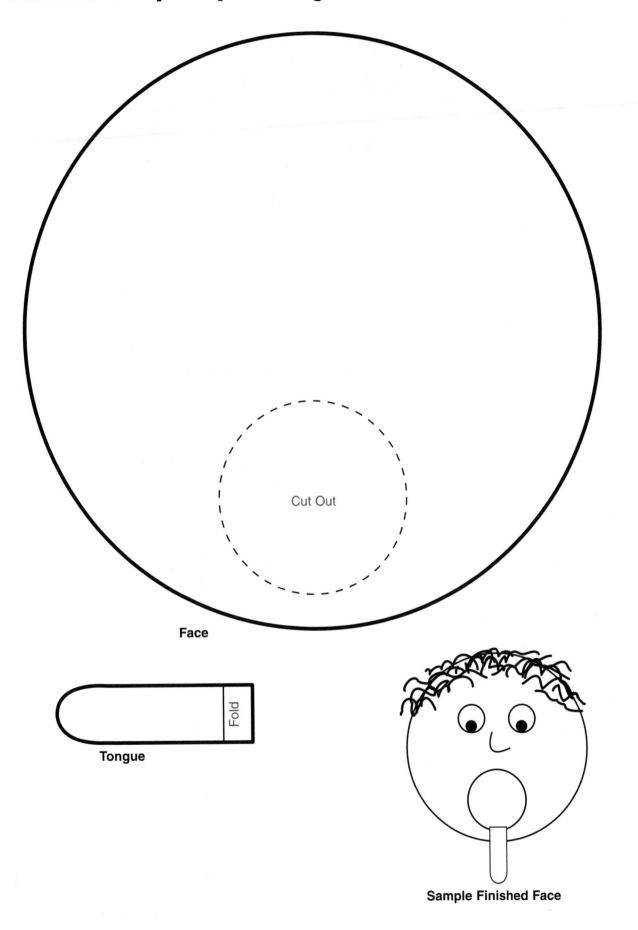

Face

Tongue

Fold

Cut Out

Sample Finished Face

Name Tag Patterns for Feel Better Stories

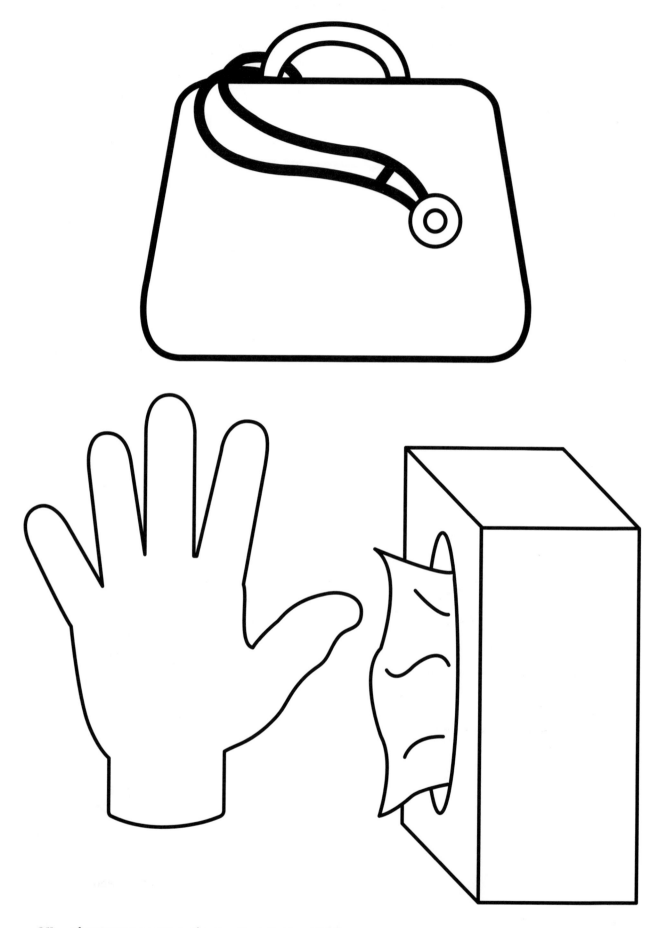

Fall Fun
Apples, Popcorn and Pumpkins

Before Storytime

Name Tags

Copy the name tag patterns on page 44. Make enough copies so you have one name-tag per child. Cut the name tags out and color them if you like. Pin the name tag to the child's shirt or punch a hole in it and string it with yarn for a necklace.

Props

- Fill a basket with three colors of apples, a small pumpkin and an ear of corn. Plastic fruits and vegetables work well. Cover the basket to add some mystery. If you can, juggle the various fruits and vegetables.

Storytime

- Introduce the theme by asking children about their name tags. If your name tags are apples, ask them what color they are. Ask, "Are there other colors of apples?" "What color are pumpkins?" "What color are they as they grow?" "Would you want a green pumpkin to make a pie or jack-o'-lantern?"

- Ask the children to name the fruits and vegetables you brought. Ask, "What do we do with them?"

- Sing the storytime song on page 7.

- Intersperse stories, fingerplays, songs and activities to fit your theme and time frame.

Apple Snacks

Serve apple slices and warm or cold apple-sauce. Discuss the ways apples can be warm such as apple pie, applesauce, apple cake and apple muffins.

Apple Muffins

Ingredients:

- 1½ cup flour
- ½ cup sugar
- 1 tsp. cinnamon
- ½ tsp. nutmeg
- ½ tsp. baking soda
- ¼ tsp. baking powder
- ¼ tsp. salt
- 1 beaten egg
- ⅓ cup milk
- ⅓ cup cooking oil
- 1 cup finely chopped, peeled apple
- apple butter, cinnamon jelly or cinnamon sugar

Directions:

1. Sift together the dry ingredients. (If time is a factor, pre-mix and bag.)

2. Combine the oil, milk and egg; beat well. Add the dry ingredients; blend till moist.

3. Fold in chopped apple.

4. Spoon into muffin cups, filling ⅔ full.

5. Top with a spoonful of apple butter, cinnamon jelly or cinnamon sugar.

6. Bake at 375°F for about 18 minutes or until golden brown.

Popcorn Snack

Serve various flavors of popcorn such as cheese flavored, buttered and caramel coated. You might also try to make ranch or taco-flavored popcorn by adding prepackaged ranch or taco seasoning mix.

Note: If using a hot air popper you will need to add butter to make the seasoning stick.

Pumpkin Snack

Serve roasted pumpkin seeds.

Pumpkin Muffins

Ingredients:

- 2 cups flour
- ½ cup sugar
- 2 tsps. baking powder
- 1 tsp. ground cinnamon
- ½ tsp. ground nutmeg
- ¼ tsp. salt
- ¼ tsp. ground mace
- ¼ tsp. ground allspice
- 1 beaten egg
- ¾ cup milk
- ½ cup canned pumpkin
- ¼ cup cooking oil
- ¼ cup packed brown sugar
- crumb topping *(optional)*

Directions:

1. Mix together the dry ingredients. (If time is a factor, pre-mix and bag.)

2. Mix together egg, milk, pumpkin and oil. Stir in dry ingredients until moistened (batter should be lumpy).

3. Spoon into muffin cups, filling ⅔ full.

4. Crumb Topping: combine ¼ cup flour, ¼ cup packed brown sugar and 2 tbsps. melted margarine. Mix until crumbly. Sprinkle muffins with topping, if desired.

5. Bake at 400°F for 20–25 minutes.

Discussion Questions

Ask specific questions to reinforce comprehension concepts.

For example:

- "Were you tricked by the apple in the book *Who's Got the Apple?*"

- "Do you think Popcorn Nell from *The Popcorn Shop* will have the same problems with pizza as she did with her popcorn?"

Wrapping It Up

Sing the goodbye song on page 8.

Songs

General Fall Songs

Fall Song

Sung to the tune: "Row, Row, Row, Your Boat"

Fall, fall, fall's the time,
For squash and pumpkin pie.
Apples, popcorn, jack-o'-lanterns,
Colored leaves blow by!

Fall, fall, fall's the time,
For leaves of red and brown.
Merrily, merrily, merrily, merrily,
Leaves are falling down.

It's Fall Time

Sung to the tune: "It's Raining, It's Pouring"

It's fall time,
(Spread arms out wide.)
It's our time.
(Point to self.)
For apples, popcorn, pumpkins.
(Rub tummy.)
It's so great, don't hesitate,
(Wiggle finger.)
Let's pop corn and carve pumpkins.
(Pretend to carve a pumpkin.)

I'm bobbing for apples,
(Put hands behind back and bend at the waist.)

Yellow, green and red ones.
Jack-o'-lantern's watching me,
(Place fingers in circle over eyes.)
Which one will I pick, let's see.
(Shrug shoulders.)

Autumn Leaves

Sung to the tune: "London Bridges"

(Use as a flannel board song or pass out a colored construction paper leaf to each child. Stand and drop arms or leaves towards the ground.)

Autumn leaves are falling down,
Falling down, falling down.
Autumn leaves are falling down,
To the ground!

Autumn leaves are falling down,
Falling down, falling down.
Autumn leaves are falling down,
All around town!

Apple Songs

Favorite Pie Song

Sung to the tune: "Skip to My Lou"

(Child's name) likes apple pie, my oh my.
(Child's name) likes apple pie, my oh my.
(Child's name) likes apple pie, my oh my.
Clap if you like apple pie!

Note: *Change child's name and pie names. Can also change "pie" to "popcorn."*

Do You Know the Apple Man?

Sung to the tune: "Muffin Man"

Do you know the apple man,
The apple man, the apple man?
Do you know the apple man,
Who likes to play with me?

Oh, he has a great big smile,
A great big smile, a great big smile.
Oh, he has a great big smile,
And likes to play with me.

Oh, he has a bright red face,
A bright red face, a bright red face.
Oh, he has a bright red face,
And likes to play with me.

Oh, he has a star inside,
A star inside, a star inside.
Oh, he has a star inside,
And likes to play with me.

Apple Pie

Sung to the tune: "Alouette"

Apples, apples,
Yellow, juicy apples.
Apples, apples,
You'll be in a pie.

Sprinkled sugar,
Cinnamon and nutmeg,
Make the yummy recipe taste just right.

Apples, apples,
Juicy, yellow apples.
Apples, apples,
Make delicious pie.

Additional verses: *red and green.*

A Little Apple Seed

Sung to the tune: "Eensy Weensy Spider"

Once a little apple seed,
(Hold fingers together to show a small seed.)
Was planted in the ground.
(Place on the ground.)
Down came the raindrops,
(Feather fingers to show rain.)
Falling all around.

Out came the big sun,
(Form a circle for the sun.)
Bright as bright could be.
And that little apple seed,
Grew to be an apple tree.
(Raise arms to make a tree.)

Sing a Song of Apples

Sung to the tune: "Sing a Song of Sixpence"
(Use with Gross Motor Skills Activity on page 40.)

All: Sing a song of apples 1, 2, 3.

Teacher sings: (Child or children's name) can you find number 1 for me?

(Name two children at once if you have more than ten children.)

All: Sing a song of apples 1, 2, 3.

Teacher sings: (Name) can you find number 2 for me?

All: Sing a song of apples 1, 2, 3.

Teacher sings: (Name) can you find number 3 for me?

(Continue with 4, 5, 6 and 7, 8, 9, etc.)

All: Sing a song of apples there's still number 10.

Teacher sings: (Name) can you find number 10 for me?

All: Sing a song of apples, see our tree? Apple picking is as fun as can be!

Note: Use the numbers from the song as a transition for another activity such as washing for snack or beginning a new group activity.

Apples are a Rockin'

Sung to the tune: "Shortening Bread"
This is a positional language game.

Apples are a rockin', rockin', rockin',
Apples are a rockin' to our song.
Apples are a rockin', rockin', rockin',
Apples are a rockin' up and down.

(Continue with behind our backs, high and low, side-to-side, etc.)

Popcorn Songs

Popcorn

Sung to the tune: "Pop Goes the Weasel"

Whir goes the popper noise.
Click-clack go the kernels.
Now we're waiting, when will it start?
Pop! Goes the popcorn!

Popcorn

Sung to the tune: "Frére Jacques"

I am popcorn.
I am popcorn.
In the pan,
In the pan,
Watch me start hopping,
Watch me start popping.
(Have the children hop up and down.)
Here I go,
Pop, pop, pop! *(Clap.)*

Pumpkin Songs

Orange Pumpkin

Sung to the tune: "I'm a Little Teapot"

I'm an orange pumpkin, fat and round,
(Form circle with hands.)
Growing in a field on the ground.
(Point to ground.)
I'll be a jack-o'-lantern with two big eyes,
(Form two circles with fingers.)
Or maybe baked into two fat pies!
(Form big circle with arms.)

The Great Pumpkin

Sung to the tune: "Did You Ever See a Lassie?"

I am the great pumpkin,
Great pumpkin, great pumpkin.
I am the great pumpkin,
Come dance with me.

For your friends are my friends,
And my friends are your friends.

I am the great pumpkin,
Come dance with me!

Note: All stand in a circle and hold hands. The child in the middle is the "great pumpkin." The "great pumpkin" picks someone to dance with in the center of the circle. The dancer then becomes the "great pumpkin" and chooses someone to dance with.

Fingerplays

Apple Fingerplays

Five Little Apples

(Can be used as a flannel board story. Hold up correct number of fingers.)

Five little apples, I wish there were more,
I *(or the name of a child)* just picked one,
And now there are four.

Four little apples hanging on a tree,
I *(or the name of a child)* just picked one,
And now there are three.

Three little apples, only a few,
I *(or the name of a child)* just picked one,
And now there are two.

Two little apples hanging in the sun,
I *(or the name of a child)* just picked one,
And now there is one.

One little apple, pick it and run,
I *(or the name of a child)* did that,
And now there are none!

Way up High in the Apple Tree
Traditional

Way up high in the apple tree,
(Bring up arms to make a tree.)
Two little apples smiled at me!
(Hold two fingers together to form two apples.)
I shook that tree as hard as I could,
(Shake arms.)
And down came the apples,
(Feather fingers down.)
Mmmm, were they good!
(Rub tummy.)

Little Red Apple

A little red apple,
(Form circle with hands.)
Hung high in a tree.
(Reach up.)
I looked up at it,
(Look up.)
And it looked down at me.
(Look down.)

"Come down, please," I called.
(Cup hands to mouth.)
And what do you suppose?
That little red apple,
(Form circle with hands.)
Dropped right on my nose!
(Point to nose.)

Pumpkin Fingerplay and Poem

Five Little Pumpkins *Traditional*

Five little pumpkins sitting on a gate.
(Hold up appropriate fingers.)

The first one said, "My it's getting late!"

The second one said, "There's a chill in the air!"

The third one said, "But we don't care!"

The fourth one said, "I'm ready for some fun!"

The fifth one said, "Let's run, run, run!"

Then oooooo went the wind and out *(clap)* went the lights,

And the five little pumpkins rolled out of sight.

My Jack-o'-Lantern

I laugh at my jack-o'-lantern.
I think he is funny to see.
He must be thinking the same thing,
Cause he's laughing at me!

Activities

Apple Activities

Apple Seeds
Supplies needed:

- apple seeds (save ahead of time and let dry)
- paper plate
- scissors
- red, green, yellow and brown construction paper

- glue
- hole punch

Directions:

1. Use the name tag pattern on page 44 and copy the apple shape onto paper plates. Cut them out.

2. Have the children tear the construction paper into small pieces and glue them to one side of the apple. On the opposite side, glue the apple seeds to show what the inside of an apple looks like.

3. Use a hole punch to punch through the apple several times so it looks like a worm chewed through the apple. The children can stick their fingers through the hole so there is a "worm" in their apple.

Gross Motor Skills Activity

Draw a tree on a large piece of paper or a chalkboard. Use the apple pattern on page 44 to make one apple for each child. Number the apples one to ten. If you have more than ten children make two of each number until you have the proper amount. Place the apples on the tree with poster putty. Sing "Sing a Song of Apples" with the children.

Apple Stamps

Supplies needed:

- apples
- paint
- cornstarch
- paper

Directions:

1. Cut the apples in various ways (horizontally, vertically, etc.) so the seeds show through.

2. Add cornstarch to the paint so that it dries faster.

3. Have the children use the apples as stamps to make a fall painting.

Science Activity

Discuss the various colors of apples and the color of the inside. Ask, "Can the seeds inside grow more seeds?" Discuss the concept of large and small and that all apples are not the same size or shape, a lot like people—we all have the same parts, but we don't all look the same. Have the children name the parts of an apple (show one that has a stem and a leaf left on it).

Fine Motor Skills Activity

Cut red, green and yellow apple shapes into puzzle pieces. Number the pieces on the back and have the children match the numbers, colors or sizes. For word recognition write the words on the back of the pieces (green apple, yellow apple, red apple) and have the children match the colors.

Popcorn Activities

Popcorn Art

Supplies needed:

- hot-air popped popcorn
- glue
- crayons or markers

Directions:

1. Use the pattern for the bowl or the corncob on page 43. Enlarge them to the desired size. Cut out one for each child.

2. Have the children glue hot-air popped popcorn onto the bowl or corncob. Then color the rest of the picture. Ask them to narrate a story about where and when they like to eat popcorn.

Popcorn Relay (Gross Motor Skills)

Play a relay race using popped popcorn on a spoon. Place movie popcorn boxes or tubs at one end of the room and have the children form two lines at the other end. Each team member must carry popcorn on their spoon to the box or tub. If time permits, have the children count the popcorn pieces that made it into the box or tub. Older children can add the two team's totals together.

Popcorn Game

Give each child a number from one to five. Form a circle with the children. One child is the "corn popper" in the middle of the circle. He or she chooses a number and calls "Pop, pop, popcorn number four." All of the children with that number go into the center of the circle and jump up and down as popcorn popping. The "corn popper" taps one of the children and he or she becomes the "corn popper."

Popcorn Painting

Supplies needed:

- paint tray
- paint
- popcorn
- kernels
- box lid
- paper

Directions:

1. Put a very small amount of paint in a paint tray. Have the children put un-popped kernels of popcorn in the tray, roll them around, then scoop them out with the spoon.

2. Place a piece of paper in a box lid for each child. Have the children put their painted kernels on the paper.

3. Carefully have them "pop" the paper by holding the box lid and jerking their hands up. If the kernels stick, tap the bottom of the box. The kernels will leave little dots of paint on the paper. Use a variety of colors to make a pretty pattern.

Science Activity

Have an ear of sweet corn available so the children can see how corn looks in its original state. Read *Tractor* by Craig Brown so the children can see how sweet corn is grown. Discuss how corn grows, what it looks like

and how it compares to sweet corn. You can also show them the stages of popcorn, starting with the kernels you buy at the store, a partially popped kernel and fully popped corn. It's surprising how many children only see the finished product!

Fine Motor Skills Activity

Number small paper cups from one to ten. Have the children count out the correct number of popcorn kernels and place them in the appropriate cups.

Pumpkin Activities

Pumpkin Bookmark

Supplies needed:

- card stock paper or thin cardboard
- scissors
- crayons or markers
- glue

Directions:

1. Cut out a bookmark for each child. Reduce the pumpkin on page 44 or use your own illustration. Make a tracer so the children can cut the pumpkins out themselves, or have the shapes already cut out. Have the children glue them to their bookmark.

2. Have the children use a black marker and add any face they wish to their jack-o'-lantern. Write "Carve out time for a good book!" on each bookmark.

3. If time permits, have the children tell you what their favorite story was that day, then write it on the back of the bookmark for them.

Pin the Face on the Pumpkin

Hang a paper pumpkin on the wall or draw one on the chalkboard. Have two eyes, a nose and a mouth cut out of black construction paper. Put poster putty on the back of the pieces. Tie a scarf around each child's eyes as they try to put the face pieces on the pumpkin. *Note: The pumpkin needs to be at room temperature for the putty to stick.*

Pass the Pumpkin

Have everyone sit in a circle. Pass a plastic or real pumpkin while you beat a drum or coffee can fast or slow. The pace of the beat determines how the pumpkin gets passed. When the beat stops, the child holding the pumpkin stands up and takes a bow or says, "Boo!"

Pumpkin Hula

Have the children try to toss a hula hoop over a pumpkin.

Science Activity

Look for a pumpkin that has a green side to show the children how a pumpkin starts out. Discuss that pumpkins grow in the ground. How is that different from an apple? How is it the same as popcorn?

Fine Motor Skills Activity

Have the children form the first letter of their name with pumpkin seeds. Older children could try to spell their first name if enough seeds are available.

Storytime Books to Share

Books About Apples

Johnny Appleseed: A Tall Tale by Steven Kellogg. Scholastic, 1989. Presents the life of John Chapman (Johnny Appleseed).

My Apple Tree by Harriet Ziefert. HarperCollins, 1991. A dog shows why he likes his apple tree.

Ten Apples Up on Top by Theo LeSieg. Random House, 1998. A story in rhyme about a number of animals who could carry ten apples on their heads.

Where's the Apple Pie? by Valeri Gorbachev. Philomel Books, 1999. A simple question leads to a more and more outlandish situation.

Who's Got the Apple? by Jan Lööf. Random House, 1975. A man buys an apple from a storekeeper who plays a joke on him, but adventures prove that the joke is on the storekeeper.

Who Stole the Apples? by Sigrid Heuck. Knopf, 1986. The adventures of a horse and bear as they try to discover who has stolen the apples from a tree.

Books About Popcorn

Popcorn by Frank Asch. Trumpet Club, 1992. Sam Bear invites his friends to an impromptu Halloween party and asks them to bring a treat.

Popcorn by Alex Moran. Harcourt Brace, 1999. A young girl and her friends make popcorn and it gets out of hand.

Popcorn at the Palace by Emily Arnold McCully. Browndeer Press, 1997. In the mid-1800s, Maisie Ferris and her father travel to England to introduce the American phenomenon of popcorn.

The Popcorn Book by Tomie de Paola. Holiday House, 1978. Presents a variety of facts about popcorn and includes two recipes.

The Popcorn Shop by Alice Low. Scholastic, 1993. To keep up with demand, Popcorn Nell buys a very large popcorn machine, but when it pops day and night, it makes far too much popcorn!

Tractor by Craig Brown. Greenwillow Books, 1995. A farmer uses his tractor to prepare the soil, plant seeds, harvest corn and haul it away to be sold.

Books About Pumpkins

The Biggest Pumpkin Ever by Steven Kroll. Scholastic, 1984. Two mice, each without the other's knowledge, help a pumpkin grow into "the biggest pumpkin ever."

The Pumpkin Man by Judith Moffatt. Scholastic, 1998. Children stuff old clothes with autumn leaves, add gloves and boots and a carved pumpkin to make a pumpkin man with a happy glowing face.

Pumpkins: A Story for a Field by Mary Lyn Ray. Harcourt, Brace, Jovanovich, 1992. A man harvests and sells a bountiful crop of pumpkins so that he will be able to preserve a field from developers.

This is the Pumpkin by Abby Levine. A. Whitman, 1997. A cumulative rhyme that describes the activities of Max, his younger sister and other children as they celebrate Halloween at school.

Patterns for Popcorn Activities

Enlarge to desired size.

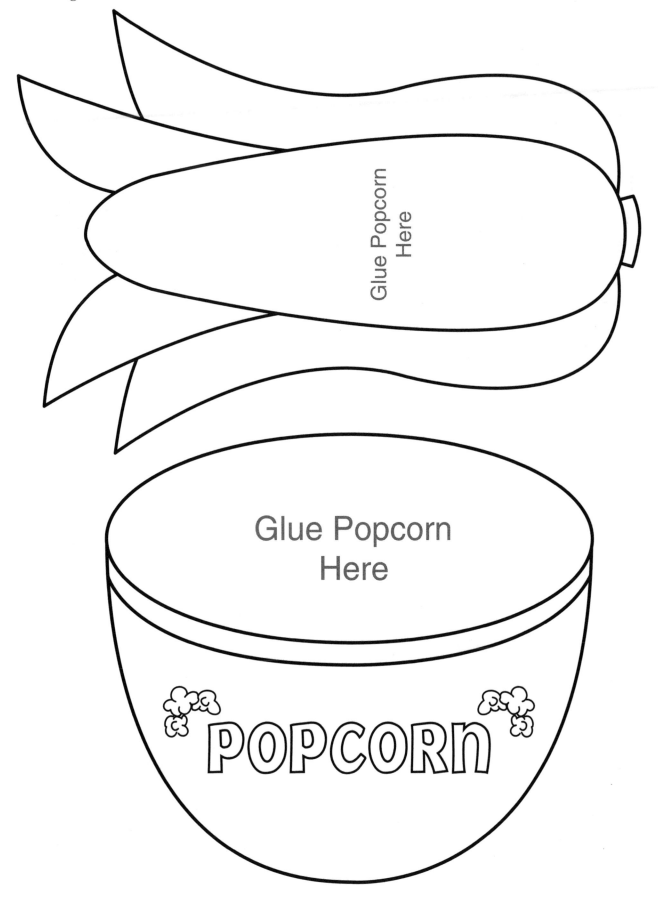

Glue Popcorn Here

Glue Popcorn Here

POPCORN

Name Tag Patterns for Fall Fun

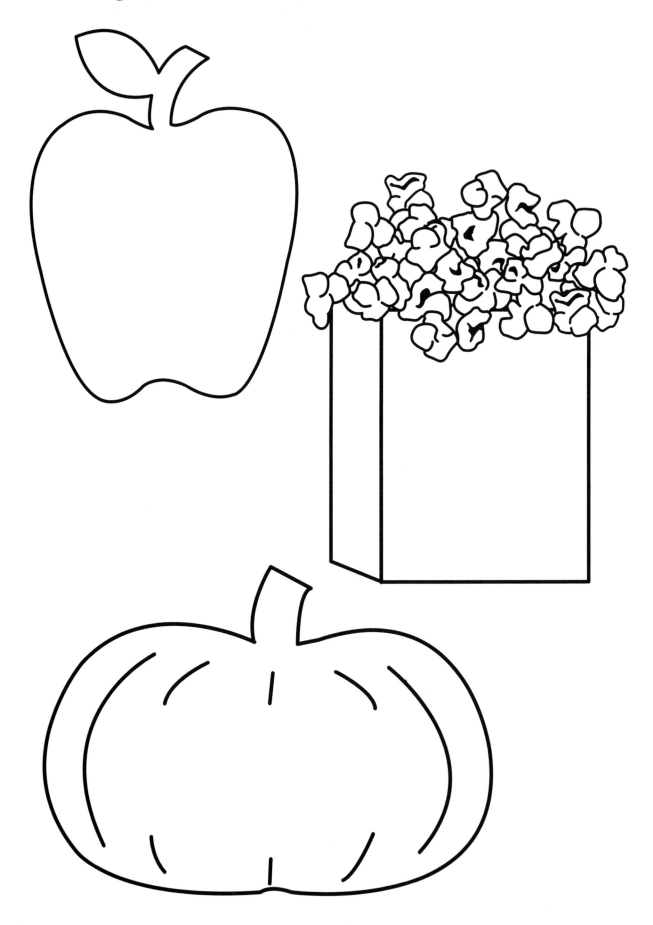

Wiggly Good Tales

Worms, Bugs and Spiders

Before Storytime

Name Tags

Copy the name tag patterns on page 51. Make enough copies so you have one name tag per child. Cut the name tags out and color them if you like. Pin the name tag to the child's shirt or punch a hole in it and string it with yarn for a necklace.

Props

- worm puppet (Cut a finger from a glove and glue on wiggle eyes or draw a face on it.)

- bug puppet (See page 49. Or use an old headband and add pipe cleaners with small Styrofoam balls for antennas.)

- picnic basket for your books (Spread out a blanket and have the children sit around you as you tell the stories.)

Storytime

- Introduce the theme by asking the children about their name tags.

- Ask, "Do you like worms? "Have you ever heard any worm stories?" "What do we use worms for?" "What creatures eat worms?" "What kind of bugs have you seen, do you like bugs?" "Why do we have bugs?" "Where do we see bugs?" "Do you think bugs talk?"

- Sing the storytime song on page 7.

- Intersperse stories, fingerplays, songs and activities that fit your theme and time frame.

Worm Snack

Serve pudding with crushed chocolate cookies and gummy worms on top.

Bug Snack

Have the children build their own "ants on a log." Spread celery sticks with peanut butter and add raisins for the ants.

Discussion Questions

Ask specific questions to reinforce comprehension concepts.

For example:

- "Would you attend a spider's tea party like in the book *Miss Spider's Tea Party*?"

- "What if you were another bug and you were asked to a spider's tea party?"

- "Do you think all ladybugs are grouchy like in the book *The Very Grouchy Ladybug*?"

- "Did you know ants worked as hard as they did in the book *The Ant Bully*?"

Wrapping It Up

Sing the goodbye song on page 8.

Songs

Spider Song

The Itsy Bitsy Spider

The itsy bitsy spider,
Climbed up the water spout.
Down came the rain,
And washed the spider out.

Out came the sun,
And dried up all the rain.
And the itsy, bitsy spider,
Went down the spout again.

Now the spider sat upon the ground,
And wondered what to do.

So the itsy, bitsy spider,
Climbed outside the water spout.
Down came the rain,
But it didn't wash her out.
She climbed and she climbed,
And she made it all the way,
And began to spin a web,
Where it wouldn't get washed away.

Bug Songs

The Ants Go Marching *Traditional*

Sung to the tune: "When Johnny Comes Marching Home"

The ants go marching one by one,
Hurrah! Hurrah!
The ants go marching one by one,
Hurrah! Hurrah!
The ants go marching one by one,
The little one stops to suck his thumb,
And we all go marching down,
To the ground, to get out of the rain.
Boom, boom, boom.

The ants go marching two by two, etc.
The little one stops to tie his shoe, etc.

The ants go marching three by three, etc.
The little one stops to climb a tree, etc.

Bumble Bee

Sung to the tune: "Jingle Bells"

Bumble bee, bumble bee,
Landing on my nose.
Bumble bee, bumble bee,
Now he's on my toes.

On my arms, on my legs,
On my elbows.
Bumble bee, oh bumble bee,
He lands and then he goes.

A Fly is On My Toe

Sung to the tune: "The Farmer in the Dell"

A fly is on my toe.
A fly is on my toe.
Hi-ho, just watch me blow,
A fly is on my toe.

Note: *Continue with other verses—a fly is on my nose, my head, my ear, my elbow and my knee.*

Shoo Fly *Traditional*

Shoo fly, don't bother me,
Shoo fly, don't bother me,
Shoo fly, don't bother me,
For I belong to somebody!

Fingerplays

Worm Fingerplays

Where's the Wiggly, Squiggly Worm?

See the wiggly, wiggly worm,
(Wave index finger.)
See it squiggly, squiggly squirm.
(Wiggle the finger in the air.)
Over, under, all around …
(Wiggle finger over, under, around the open left hand.)
Where's the wiggly, squiggly worm?
(Hide the finger inside the left fist. Count to three and the worms "pop out.")

Wiggly Bookworm

(Use with Bug Puppets on page 49.)

There was a wiggly bookworm,
(Wiggle finger.)
Who wiggled all around.
One day he saw a dark green book,
Sitting on the ground.

"Oh, I love books," said the worm,
And opened his mouth wide.
He munched right through that book,
And peeked out the other side.

Wiggles

(Do appropriate actions as you say the rhyme.)

A wiggle wiggle here,
A wiggle wiggle there,
Wiggle your hands up in the air.
Wiggle your shoulders,
Wiggle your hips,
Wiggle your knees,
And move your lips.
Wiggle, wiggle, wiggle.
And wiggle some more—
And now let's sit down on the floor.

Inchworm

Inchworm, inchworm, inching along,
(Bend index finger and move it up and down.)

Inchworm, inchworm, singing a song.
(Hold one hand up to your ear.)

Inchworm, inchworm, before the day ends,
(Put hands in circle above head and drop arms flat.)

Inchworm, inchworm, will you be my friend?
(Put hands out, palms up.)

Spider Fingerplay

This Little Spider

This little spider went swimming,
(Make swimming motion with arms.)
This little spider played ball.
(Make ball throwing motion.)
This little spider was napping,
(Put hands together under tilted head.)
This little spider was tall.
(Stretch arms overhead.)
And this little spider went wee-wee-wee,
All the way home.
(Make running motion with fingers.)

Bug Fingerplays

Bug

1, 2, 3.
(Hold up fingers.)
There is a bug on me!

(Point to shoulder.)
Where did it go?
(Brush off.)
I don't know.
(Shrug shoulders and look puzzled.)

Bugs

(Use puppets and do appropriate actions.)

A mosquito, a spider, a ladybug,
All crawl around and bug me.
Which one of them will hurt you?
None, just say … shoo please!

If I Were an Ant

If I were an ant, I'd spend an hour,
Climbing up a lovely flower.
(Hand over hand, reaching high.)

If I were an ant, I'd go for a ride,
On the back of a dog with a long, long stride.
(Take three giant steps.)

If I were an ant, I'd look for a tree,
And climb to the top, where I could see.
(Hand on forehead, look far away.)

If I were an ant, I'd follow you home,
And hide by your table to wait for crumbs.
(Rub tummy, say "Yum!")

Activities

Worm Activities

Bookworm

Supplies needed:

- half sheet of construction paper (one for each book)
- paper
- glue or staples
- markers
- hole punch

Directions:

1. Fold the construction paper in half to make a book.

2. Cut two sheets of white paper small enough to fit inside the book. Secure them with glue or staples.

3. Depending on the children's ages, have them write a title on their book. Or write their title for them. If you like, entitle the book "How to be a Bookworm" by I. M. Aworm.

4. Punch several holes together on the back cover so it looks as though a bookworm has chewed through it. You may want to make it large enough so the children can stick their finger through it.

5. Have the children write a story and illustrate it. This can also be a take-home project.

Paint with Worms

Supplies needed:

- paint
- paper
- gummy or rubber worms

Directions:

1. Have the children use gummy or rubber fishing worms to paint designs on the paper.

2. Pass out a gummy worm to each child at the program as a treat.

Worm Race (Gross Motor Skills)

Make a worm race track on an old cookie sheet. Make row dividers out of aluminum foil and place them on the cookie sheet.

Number each lane. Let live fishing worms go and see who will get to the finish line first. Or let the children be the worms. Have them inch forward like worms. This could also be done as a team race. Discuss and demonstrate the concepts of fast and slow.

Fine Motor Skills Activity

Check at a bait or fishing shop for rubber worms of various colors. Hide them in a play table filled with dried coffee grounds. Have the children count the worms and sort them.

Math Activity

Have a contest to see who can guess how many gummy worms are in the jar.

Spider Activities

Clothespin Spiders

Supplies needed:

- black paint
- cornstarch *(optional)*
- hinged clothespins (one for each spider)
- cotton balls
- black pipe cleaners or crayons, markers or colored pencils
- toothpicks

Directions:

1. Add cornstarch to a very small amount of paint.

2. Insert a cotton ball into the mouth of the clothespin. Dip it into the black paint.

3. Glue on pipe cleaners for legs or use crayons, markers or colored pencils.

4. Use a toothpick to draw eyes and a mouth in the wet paint.

Thumbprint Spider

Have children use a washable inkpad to make thumbprints on white paper. Use a black pen to add legs and a red pen to add eyes and mouth.

Construction Paper Spiders

Supplies needed:

- black construction paper
- colored chalk
- black pipe cleaners (eight for each spider)

Directions:

1. Cut an oval shape out of black construction paper.

2. Have the children use colored chalk to draw on eyes and a mouth.

3. For the legs, poke pipe cleaners through the paper and over the spider's body. (This is a good opportunity to talk about how many legs spiders and bugs have.)

Fine Motor Skills Activity

Place numbered cards on a table. Have the children count out plastic bugs and spiders and place the appropriate number on each card. Then have them sort the bugs and spiders according to color and kind.

Science and Math Activity

Have pictures of different kinds of bugs and spiders set out on a table. Ask the children to sort the pictures according to if they fly or crawl, what color they are, if they are a spider or a bug and if they have seen them in their own house or yard. If the pictures are large enough they can count the number of spots and/or legs on each bug.

Bug Activities

Bug Puppets

Supplies needed:

- paper plates, felt or paper
- glue, tape or staples
- crayons or markers
- pipe cleaners

Directions:

1. Cut two ovals from the paper plates, felt or paper. The ovals should be bigger than your hand. Depending on the age of your children and the time allotted, you might want to pre-cut the pieces. If the children will be cutting out their own pieces, have a sturdy tracer made out of heavy cardboard so they have a pattern to follow.

2. Let the children attach the two ovals with glue, tape or staples along the edges to make the puppet. Leave one end open for your hand.

3. Cut two smaller ovals and attach them to the body for wings.

4. Have the children use crayons or markers to make spots for a ladybug or other features for different bugs.

5. Use pipe cleaners to add antennas.

Gross Motor Skills Activity

Have one child be the queen ant. He or she stands on the "anthill." The other children ask to be a big bug (1 giant step), a small bug (1 regular step) or a spider (8 baby steps). Demonstrate these steps ahead of time. Whoever reaches the anthill first becomes the queen ant.

Storytime Books to Share

Books About Worms

The Big Fat Worm by Nancy Van Laan. Knopf, 1987. A rhythmic tale describing a chain of events set in motion when a big fat bird tries to eat a big fat worm.

Grandpas are for Finding Worms by Harriet Ziefert. Puffin Books, 2000. When you need worms for fishing, Grandpa knows just where to look. Grandpas are great at making things, like bookshelves, burgers and funny faces. Some grandpas like to sing old songs, some like to play baseball and all grandpas make you feel special.

Inch by Inch by Leo Lionni. Mulberry Books, 1995. In this classic book, a winsome inchworm is proud of his ability to measure anything under the sun.

Loon Lake Fishing Derby by Kathleen Cook Waldron. Orca Book Publishers, 1999. When Loon Lake holds a fishing derby, entrepreneurial Wally starts selling worms. But things quickly get out of hand as floods of fishermen descend and hordes of other worm sellers dig up gardens around town.

Worms Wiggle by David Pelham and Michael Foreman. Simon & Schuster Books for Young Readers, 1988. Worms wiggle and bugs jiggle; frogs leap and caterpillars creep in this richly painted and cleverly engineered pop-up book that focuses on how creatures get from here to there.

Wormy Worm by Christopher Raschka. Hyperion Books, 2000. As Wormy Worm wiggles and woggles, it's hard to tell which end is front and which end is back.

Books About Spiders

Dance, Spider, Dance! by Robert Kraus. Western Pub. Co., 1993. Spider wants to enter a dance contest but can't dance. With the help of his friends fly and ladybug, some exciting surprises occur.

Eency Weency Spider by Joanne Oppenheim. Gareth Stevens Pub., 1997. After climbing the water spout, Eency Weency Spider meets Little Miss Muffet, Humpty Dumpty and Little Jack Horner.

Fresh Cider and Pie by Franz Brandenberg. Macmillan, 1973. A fly outwits a spider by making apple cider and pie.

The Itsy Bitsy Spider by Iza Trapani. Whispering Coyote Press, 1993. The itsy bitsy spider encounters a fan, a mouse, a cat and a rocking chair as she makes her way to the top of a tree to spin her web.

The Lady and the Spider by Faith McNulty. Harper & Row, 1986. A spider who lives in a head of lettuce is saved when the lady who finds her puts her back in the garden.

Miss Spider's Tea Party by David Kirk. Scholastic, 1994. Wary insects do not dare stop by Miss Spider's for tea, but when a wayward moth falls into one of Miss Spider's cups, she graciously rescues it and soon finds herself surrounded by new friends.

Sophie's Masterpiece: A Spider's Tale by Eileen Spinelli. Simon & Schuster Books for Young Readers, 2001. Sophie the spider makes wondrous webs, but the residents of Beekman's Boarding House do not appreciate her until at last, old and tired, she weaves her final masterpiece.

Spiders in the Fruit Cellar by Barbara Joose. Knopf, 1983. Elisabeth is old enough to go to the fruit cellar alone, but she is afraid of spiders lurking there.

The Very Busy Spider by Eric Carle. Philomel Books, 1984. The farm animals try to divert a busy little spider from spinning her web, but she persists and produces a thing of both beauty and usefulness.

Books About Bugs

The Ant Bully by John Nickle. Scholastic, 1999. Lucas learns a lesson about bullying when he is pulled into the ant hole he has been tormenting.

The Grouchy Ladybug by Eric Carle. Harper Festival, 1999. Progressing through a series of brilliantly colored die-cut pages, a bad-tempered braggart becomes a nicer, happier, better-behaved bug.

I Know an Old Lady Who Swallowed a Fly illustrated by Glen Rounds. Holiday House, 1990. A cumulative folk song in which the solution is worse than the predicament when an old lady swallows a fly.

I Know an Old Lady Who Swallowed a Fly retold by Nadine Bernard Westcott. Little, Brown, 1980. A retelling of the classic tale.

Ladybug, Ladybug by Ruth Brown. Dutton Children's Books, 1988. In this adaptation of the familiar nursery rhyme, Ladybug encounters a variety of animals while rushing home to her children.

There Was an Old Lady Who Swallowed a Fly illustrated by Pam Adams. Child's Play International Ltd., 1990. Presents the traditional song with illustrations on die-cut pages that reveal all the old lady swallows.

Two Bad Ants by Chris Van Allsburg. Houghton Mifflin, 1988. Two wayward ants decide to return to the safety of their colony after some harrowing experiences.

The Very Lonely Firefly by Eric Carle. Penguin Putnam, 1999. A firefly discovers many different kinds of lights as he searches for other fireflies.

The Very Quiet Cricket by Eric Carle. Philomel Books, 1990. A cricket tries very hard to return the greetings of other animals, but remains silent until he finally learns to chirp.

Why Mosquitoes Buzz in People's Ears retold by Verna Aardema. Dial Books for Young Readers, 1975. Reveals the meaning of the mosquito's buzz.

Other Media to Share

The Very Hungry Caterpillar and Other Stories. Walt Disney Home Video, 1995. Videocassette, 37 minutes.

Name Tag Patterns for Wiggly Good Tales

Count on Books

ABC's, Colors, Numbers, Shapes and School

Before Storytime

Name Tags

Copy the name tag patterns on page 61. Make enough copies so you have one name tag per child. Cut the name tags out and color them if you like. Pin the name tag to the child's shirt or punch a hole in it and string it with yarn for a necklace.

Props

- different shapes cut from various colors of construction paper
- cards with letters and numbers written on them

Storytime

As you or the children enter the room sing:

Hello Song

Sung to the tune: "Allouette"

Hello!
Hello!
How are you today-o?

Hello!
Hello!
I'm fine, Hope you are too!

- Pass out the cards and shapes.
- Ask the children about their shapes and letters or numbers. "What color are they?" "What do you think the stories might be about today?" "What is on your name tags?" "Can you learn about colors, numbers, shapes and letters at school?" "Do you know you can find these things in storybooks, too?"

- Sing the storytime song on page 7.

- Intersperse stories, fingerplays, songs and activities that fit your theme and time frame.

Snack

Serve peanut butter and jelly sandwiches cut from cookie cutters in various shapes. Or, think of things that begin with A–B–C, such as apple juice, bananas and crackers.

Discussion Questions

Ask specific questions to reinforce comprehension concepts.

For example:

- "Did you know that blue and yellow make green before we read *Warthog's Paint* and *White Rabbit's Color Book*?"

- "In the story *Hold the Bus!*, what animal got on the bus and brought the fleas?"

- "Do you think teachers have a lot of work to do to get ready for school like Miss Bindergarten in *Miss Bindergarten Gets Ready for Kindergarten*?"

Wrapping It Up

Sing the goodbye song on page 8.

Songs

ABC Songs

Alphabet Song

Sung to the tune: "Three Blind Mice"

A, B, C—A, B, C.
Sing with me—A, B, C.

A is for apples we love to eat,
B is for boots we wear on our feet,
C is for candy that tastes so sweet.
A, B, C—A, B, C.

ABC School Chant

Sung to the tune: "Marine's Marching Cadence"

A B C D E
School is where I want to be.

F G H I J
Learning to read and write each day.

K L M N O
Boys and girls I want to know.

P Q R S T
Sharing books with you and me.

U V W X Y
Now it's time to say goodbye.

Z Z Z Z Z
School is where I want to be.

Counting Songs

Count to Ten

Sung to the tune: "This Old Man"

One-two-three,
Count with me.
It's as easy as can be,
Four-five-six-seven-eight, nine, ten,
Now let's count all over again!

Counting Can Be So Much Fun

Sung to the tune: "Row, Row, Row, Your Boat"

One, two, three, four, five,
(Hold up correct number of fingers as you count.)
Six, seven, eight, nine, ten.

Counting can be so much fun,
Let's do it all again! *(Clap!)*

Count Our Numbers

Sung to the tune: "Oh My Darling Clementine"

Count our numbers,
Count our numbers,
Count our numbers, everyday.
It is fun to count our numbers,
On our fingers and our toes.

One, two, three, four,
Five, six, seven, eight,
Nine, ten we'll count today.
It is fun to count together,
On our fingers and our toes.

Count to Three

Sung to the tune: "Mary Had a Little Lamb"

Lightly tap your foot two times,
Foot two times, foot two times.
Lightly tap your foot two times,
Now let's count to three.

1, 2, 3, let's all sit down,
All sit down, all sit down.
1, 2, 3, let's all sit down,
Quietly on the ground.

Numbers March Right In

Sung to the tune: "When the Saints Go Marching In"

Oh, when the numbers, march right in,
Oh, when the numbers march right in.
We will count them one by one,
When the numbers march right in.

Oh, one-two-three and four-five-six,
And seven-eight and nine and ten.
When we finish all our numbers,
We will count them once again.

Step One, Step Two

(You may wish to end with this as a way to lead your group to the door.)

Step one! Step two!
I'm up with you!
Step three! Step four!

Let's walk some more.

Step five and six and seven and eight,
And now we're going through the gate!

Just two steps more,
We're at the door!
Step nine and ten,
We're home again!

Shapes and Colors Songs

The Triangle Song

Sung to the tune: "Pop! Goes the Weasel"

I am a small triangle. *(Show triangle shape.)*
I have three sides you see.
I also have three corners.
They're just right for me.

What Shape is This?

Sung to the tune: "The Muffin Man"

Do you know what shape this is,
(Show appropriate shapes.)
What shape this is, what shape this is?
Do you know what shape this is,
I'm holding in my hand?

Painting Fun

Sung to the tune: "Twinkle, Twinkle, Little Star"
Use props with this song if you can.

I know colors for painting fun,
Green like grass and yellow sun.
An orange pumpkin and white snow,
A red rose and a black crow,
Blue like a mailbox, brown like an ape,
A pink pig and some purple grapes.

Rainbow Song

Sung to the tune: "Hush Little Baby"

(Make rainbow arches of each color from felt and place on a flannel board. Hold up appropriate color as you sing. Or have children hold each color of construction paper and step forward as their color is mentioned.)

Rainbow purple,
Rainbow blue,
Rainbow green,
And yellow, too.
Rainbow orange,
Rainbow red,
Rainbow shining over our head.

(If the children are holding the colors, hold up over their heads or make an arch with your arms over your head.)

Come and count,
(Wave hand inward as if to beckon.)
The colors with me.
How many colors can you see?
1-2-3 on down to green,
(Hold up number of fingers as you count.)
4-5-6 colors can be seen.

Rainbow purple, *(Repeat above actions.)*
Rainbow blue,
Rainbow green,
And yellow, too.
Rainbow orange,
Rainbow red,
Rainbow shining over our head.

If You are Wearing ...

Sung to the tune: "If You're Happy and You Know It"

If you are wearing red, shake your head.
If you are wearing red, shake your head.
If you are wearing red,
Then please shake your head.
If you are wearing red, shake your head.

Other verses:

Blue, touch your shoe.

Black, pat your back.

Green, bow like a queen.

Yellow, shake like Jell-O.

Brown, turn around.

Pink, give us a wink.

Learning and School Songs

We Can Learn

Sung to the tune: "A Hunting We Will Go"

We can learn our shapes and colors.
We can learn our shapes and colors.
We're smart we've got a start,
We can learn our shapes and colors.

Additional verses repeat as above:

We can learn our ABC's …
We can learn our numbers, too …
We can learn it all with books …

I Like School

Sung to the tune: "Skip to My Lou"

I like school, oh yes I do!
I like school, oh yes I do!
I like school, oh yes I do!
We learn so many things there.

Shapes and colors, letters, too,
Numbers and who's in a zoo.
How to play and how to share,
I do lots of fun stuff there.

Paint and color, cut and glue,
Make neat things for me and you.
School is fun will you come too?
I love school, oh yes I do!

This is What We Do at School

This is the way we go to school,
Go to school, go to school.
This is the way we go to school,
So early in the morning.

This is the way we paint a picture …
(Do appropriate actions.)

This is the way we play outside …

This is the way we count to three …

This is the way we build with blocks …

This is the way we eat our snack …

Fingerplays

Three Balls

A ball,
(Join fingers to make a circle.)
A bigger ball,
(Do as above but show as larger.)
A great big ball I see!
(Form even bigger ball with hands.)
Now let's count the balls we've made,
(Make each ball as you count.)
1, 2, 3!

First Day of School

What fun it is to go to school!
(Spread arms wide.)
We'll learn so many things.
Of books and bees,
(Open hands like a book; move index finger independently as a bee.)
And flowering trees,
(Point high to "trees.")
And cockatoos with wings. *(Flap arms.)*

I am a preschooler.
(Point to self.)
I'm three or four years old.
(Hold up fingers.)
But I can learn,
(Point to self.)
And in my turn,
Be wise and strong and bold.
(Grab lapels of shirt and stick chest out.)

School

School is a happy place.
(Outstretch arms.)
Each child wears a happy face.
(Fingers to corners of mouth—smile.)
There are books and toys and lots of space.
(Spread hands.)
There they play games or have a race.
(Move two fingers as if running.)
We make so many new friends at school.
(Point to children.)
We share with them because that's the rule.
(Shake finger.)

Five Preschool Children

Five preschool children in a row.
(Hold up five fingers.)
The first one is wearing a bright red bow.
(Place hands at neck and form a bow.)
The second one has a new blue cap.
(Point to head.)
The third one's hands are in his lap.
(Place folded hands in lap.)
The fourth one says, "It's a nice day."
(Hold up four fingers.)
The fifth one met a friend on the way.
(Hold up five fingers.)
Who is that friend so new?
Is that friend you?
(Point to children.)

Activities

ABC Activities

Alphabet Soup

Read *Eating the Alphabet* by Lois Ehlert or *Alphabet Soup* by Kate Banks. Then make a bowl of alphabet soup.

Supplies needed:

- construction paper
- alphabet macaroni
- glue
- scissors
- markers or crayons

Directions:

1. Draw or trace a large circle on a piece of construction paper. Cut directly down the center to form two half circles.

2. Have the children glue the alphabet macaroni letters in their "bowl" of soup. They may use the letters to spell their name, or randomly add the letters as they are found in alphabet soup.

3. They can use the markers or crayons to add vegetables or meat to the soup and color in the liquid.

Alphabet Obstacle Course (Gross Motor Skills)

Read *ABC Cat* by Nancy Jewell or *Albert's Alphabet* by Leslie Tryon. Then run through an alphabet obstacle course.

Set up chairs, tables and any small objects to create an obstacle course. Set it up so that the children must go around, in, out, over, under, up, down and through. Discuss these concepts as you show the children the way through the maze. Hold up a letter on a card. The children whose first names begin with that letter go through the maze one by one. If you like, place alphabet cards at the end of each obstacle course. The children pick up one card as they complete the course. Then they name the letter or step forward when you call it out.

Fine Motor Skills Activity

Use paper lunch bags to create alphabet bags. Write the letter of the alphabet in upper and lower case letters on both sides of the bag. Collect small items that begin with that letter to place inside the bag. The more items in the bag the better. Include a card that lists all the items in each bag (so you know what you have in the bag and so the children have word association with each item). If you prefer, have a separate card for each item so the children can try to match the word with the item.

Counting Activities

Number Book

Read *Hold the Bus! A Counting Book from 1 to 10* by Arlene Alda, *Snoopy's 1, 2, 3* by Nancy Hall or *Look Whooo's Counting* by Suse MacDonald.

Supplies needed:

- half sheet of white paper
- washable inkpad
- crayons or markers
- scrap paper
- glue

- stickers or a stamper
- wet and dry paper towel for wiping fingers

Directions:

1. Fold the half sheet of paper horizontally, so it resembles a book.

2. Write "My Number Book" on the cover.

3. On the inside, dot the numbers 1, 2 and 3 in large slashes, each on their own page.

4. Have the children use their fingers and the inkpad to complete the number by tracing over the dashed lines to form the numbers.

5. Have the children use crayons or markers to draw one thing on the number 1 page. (You may need to suggest an object to speed things up.) On the number 2 page, have the children glue two pieces of scrap paper to represent two objects. On the number 3 page, offer three stickers that they may place on the page. Or give them the inkpad and a stamper and have them stamp three times, counting with them as they stamp.

Math Activity

Use blocks, wooden rulers or other items to measure things around your room. Have the children tell you in advance what items will need the most blocks (or other measuring item) to match its length. Ask why they chose the number they did. Also ask, "Does one item appear longer than another?" "If it is longer, would that require it to need more or fewer blocks?"

Shapes and Color Activities

Color Changes

Read *White Rabbit's Color Book* by Alan Baker or *Warthogs Paint* by Pamela Duncan Edwards. Then let the children paint with watercolors to experiment with their own color combinations. Discuss how White Rabbit changed color when he went from one color to the next. Show the book and ask the children if they can come up with the same colors that White Rabbit did.

Supplies needed:

- watercolor paint
- white paper
- paintbrushes

Directions:

1. Set the paints, paintbrushes and paper up on a table.

2. Have the children paint and experiment with the watercolors.

Color Beanbag Toss (Gross Motor Skills)

Read *Brown Bear, Brown Bear, What Do You See?* by Bill Martin Jr. or *Cat's Colors* by Jane Cabrera.

Place various colored pieces of construction paper in a scattered pattern on the floor. Have the children line up single file. Show everyone a color using a matching piece of construction paper. Have the children say the name of the color, then pass the first child in line a beanbag to toss it on that color. Continue with each child and repeat if you have the time.

Sorting Fun

Have buttons, card chips (poker), milk caps of various colors or marbles available for the children to count and sort by color.

Teacher Says Shapes

Play "Teacher Says" a version of "Simon Says." Cut different shapes out of construction paper. Make sure each child has a shape. Use positional terms to place the shapes on different body parts, the floor, etc. Separate directions into groups, for example, "Teacher says **triangles only** place your shape under your foot."

Gross Motor Skills Activity

Use the shapes, letters and numbers from the beginning of the program and scatter them on the floor in a path-like pattern. Play a version of "Mother May I?" with the children at one end of the cards and you at the other. Have the children form a line, then ask if they may take baby, regular or giant steps towards a card on the floor. They need to name the shape, letter or number of the card. Use this game to help the children with spatial concepts. For example, could they really reach the requested card with the two baby steps they asked to take?

Storytime Books to Share

Books About the ABC's

ABC Cat by Nancy Jewell. Harper & Row, 1983. A cat's antics throughout the day take him through the alphabet.

ABC Pigs Go to Market by Ida DeLage. Garrard Publishing Company, 1977. A mother pig and her little pigs go on a shopping trip and encounter everything from A to Z.

The Accidental Zucchini: An Unexpected Alphabet by Max Grover. Browndeer Press, 1993. Each letter of the alphabet is represented by an unusual combination of objects such as "fork fence," "octopus overalls" and "umbrella underwear."

Albert's Alphabet by Leslie Tryon. Atheneum, 1991. Clever Albert uses all the supplies in his workshop to build an alphabet for the school playground.

Alphabet City by Stephen T. Johnson. Viking, 1995. Paintings of objects in an urban setting present the letters of the alphabet.

Alphabet Soup by Kate Banks. Knopf, 1988. A boy's ability to spell words with his alphabet soup comes in handy during the magical journey he takes in his mind with a friendly bear.

Alphabet Under Construction by Denise Fleming. Henry Holt, 2002. A mouse works his way through the alphabet as he folds the "F," measures the "M" and rolls the "R."

A My Name is Alice by Jane Bayer. Dial Books for Young Readers, 1984. The well-known jump rope ditty that is built on letters of the alphabet is illustrated with animals from all over the world.

Baby Bop's ABC Book by Mark Bernthal. Barney Publishing, 1993. Baby Bop plays with familiar objects representing the letters of the alphabet.

Dr. Seuss's ABC: An Amazing Alphabet Book by Dr. Seuss. Random House, 1996. A rhyming text celebrating the alphabet.

Eating the Alphabet: Fruits and Vegetables From A to Z by Lois Ehlert. Harcourt, Brace, Jovanovich, 1989. An alphabetical tour of the world of fruits and vegetables, from apricot and artichoke to yam and zucchini.

Four Famished Foxes and Fosdyke by Pamela Duncan Edwards. HarperCollins, 1995. An alliterative tale about four foxes who go hunting in the barnyard while their gourmet brother fixes a vegetarian feast. A great letter "F" tongue twister tale!

Little Ernie's ABC's by Anna Ross. Random House, 1992. Little Ernie goes through the alphabet with his Sesame Street friends.

Muppet Babies Nursery Rhymes ABC by Michaela Muntean. Grolier, 1992. Short verses of nursery rhymes from A to Z.

My First ABC by Marie-Agnés Gaudrat and Thierry Courtin. Barron's Educational Series, 1994. Children illustrate both the capital and lower case letters of the alphabet in ways that show body movements to form the shapes.

Old Black Fly by Jim Aylesworth. Henry Holt & Co., 1992. Rhyming text follows a mischievous old black fly through the alphabet as he has a very bad day landing where he should not be.

Snoopy's ABC's by Nancy Hall. Golden Books, 1987. Snoopy and the gang go through the letters A to Z.

What Pete Ate from A- Z by Maira Kalman. Putnam, 2001. In this alphabet book a child relates some of the unusual things eaten by Pete the Dog.

Books About Numbers and Counting

Counting On Calico by Phyllis Limbacher Tildes. Charlesbridge Publishing, 1995. A mouse named Willy Whiskers shows how to count on the many aspects of a cat.

Each Orange Had 8 Slices: A Counting Book by Paul Giganti Jr. Greenwillow Books, 1992. An illustrated introduction to counting and simple addition.

Hold the Bus! A Counting Book from 1 to 10 by Arlene Alda. Whistle Stop Books, 1996. Introduces the numbers one through ten as the bus driver makes his rounds and picks up a usual assortment of passengers.

Let's Count It Out, Jesse Bear by Nancy White Carlstrom. Simon & Schuster, 1996. In this rhyming, rambling jaunt Jesse Bear counts to 290 showing off new shoes, bumping into bumper cars and even getting a few bumps of his own.

Little Bert's Book of Numbers by Anna Ross. Random House, 1992. Little Bert counts his favorite things from one to ten.

Little Mouse's Learn-and-Play Numbers by Anael Dena. Gareth Stevens Pub., 1997. Artwork and simple text present a variety of activities through which the reader can learn numbers.

Look Whooo's Counting by Suse MacDonald. Scholastic, 2000. Count from one to ten with wise old Owl. Join her in a moonlit flight and help find the numbers and shapes hidden in the animals she encounters.

Millions of Cats by Wanda Gag. Putnam, 1996. How can an old man and his wife select one cat from millions and trillions? A Newbery Honor Book.

One Day, Two Dragons by Lynne Bertrand. Clarkson Potter Publishers, 1992. A counting book that relates what happens when two dragons go to the doctor's office to get four vaccinations.

One Little Teddy Bear by Mark Burgess. Viking, 1991. One little teddy looking for his shoe goes through various activities and meets other bears until there are ten.

The One That Got Away by Percival Everett. Clarion, 1992. Three cowhands chase and corral ones in this zany book about the Wild West.

Rain Dance by Kathi Appelt. Harper Festival, 2001. Counting one through ten animals in the rain.

The Right Number of Elephants by Jeff Sheppard. HarperCollins, 1990. A counting book in which a little girl relies on the help of some eager elephants.

Rock It, Sock It, Number Line by Bill Martin Jr. Henry Holt & Co., 2001. Introduces the numbers one through ten as vegetables and numbers dance together at the king and queen's garden party before jumping into the soup to be eaten by a crowned boy and girl.

Snoopy's 1, 2, 3 by Nancy Hall. Golden Books, 1987. Told in rhyme, Snoopy is joined by friends for adventures that take him from one to ten.

This Old Man: The Counting Song by Robin Michal Koontz. Dodd, Mead, 1988. An illustrated version of the well-known counting song. Includes instruction accompanying play action.

Who Wants One? by Mary Serfozo. Macmillan, 1992. Rhyming text and illustrations introduce the numbers one through ten.

Books About Shapes and Colors

Brown Bear, Brown Bear, What Do You See? by Bill Martin Jr. Henry Holt & Co., 1992. Children see a variety of animals, each one a different color, and a mother looking at them.

Cat's Colors by Jane Cabrera. Dial Books for Young Readers, 1997. A cat describes ten different colors and tells which one is its favorite.

Elmer's Colors by David McKee. William Morrow & Co., 1994. Elmer the patchwork elephant helps children learn different colors.

Little Elmo's Book of Colors by Anna Ross. Random House, 1992. Little Elmo goes through a rainbow of colors with his Sesame Street friends.

Little Grover's Book of Shapes by Anna Ross. Random House, 1992. Little Grover discovers various shapes in the objects around him, including squares, triangles and stars.

Teeny, Tiny Mouse: A Book About Color by Laura Leuck. Troll Communications, 1998. A teeny, tiny mouse and his mommy point out objects of various colors all around their teeny, tiny house.

Warthogs Paint: A Messy Color Book by Pamela Duncan Edwards. Hyperion Books, 2001. As some warthogs spend a rainy day painting their kitchen, they make a mess and learn about mixing colors.

White Rabbit's Color Book by Alan Baker. Houghton Mifflin, 1994. White Rabbit hops from one paint pot to another, changing colors as he goes, until he ends up brown.

Books About Learning and School

The Day the Teacher Went Bananas by James Howe. Penguin USA, 1987. A class's new teacher, who leads the children in a number of very popular activities, turns out to be a gorilla.

Edward Unready For School by Rosemary Wells. Penguin Putnam, 1995. Edward, a shy young bear unready for play school, feels out of place surrounded by students who are ready, busy and happy.

Freddie Goes to Playgroup by Nicola Smee. Little Barron's, 1999. It's Freddie's first morning at playgroup. He is excited, but his Teddy Bear is a little scared. Soon all fears are forgotten as Freddie takes part in many activities—and discovers lots of other kids.

Froggy Goes to School by Jonathan London. Penguin Putnam, 1998. Froggy, nervous and excited about his first day of school, fumbles and jumbles about the house in an attempt to prepare himself for the approaching day.

Grover Goes to School by Dan Elliott. Random House, 1982. On the first day of school, Grover tries to please everyone but himself in order to make new friends.

Look Out Kindergarten, Here I Come! by Nancy Carlson. Penguin Putnam, 2001. Even though Henry is looking forward to going to kindergarten, he is not sure about staying once he first gets there.

Lucky Goes to School by Gail Herman. Penguin Putnam, 2001. It's the first day of school! But Lucky the puppy is worried—what will he do all day while his boy is in school?

Miss Bindergarten Gets Ready for Kindergarten by Joseph Slate. Penguin Putnam, 2001. Miss Bindergarten's soon-to-be students are excitedly, anxiously getting ready at home while Miss Bindergarten is getting ready too, gathering her gear and preparing her classroom (incorporates the alphabet within the story).

School Days by B. G. Hennessy. Penguin USA, 1992. Rhyming text and illustrations describe the familiar faces and objects of a day at school.

Timothy Goes to School by Rosemary Wells. Penguin Putnam, 2000. Timothy learns about being accepted and making friends during the first week of his first year at school.

Tiptoe Into Kindergarten by Jacquelin Rogers. Scholastic, 2003. A child tiptoes into kindergarten to see all the things they do there.

26 Letters and 99 Cents by Tana Hoban. William Morrow & Co., 1995. Color photographs of letters, numbers, coins and common objects introduce the alphabet, coinage and the counting system.

Welcome to Kindergarten by Anne Rockwell. Walker and Co., 2001. Tim visits his future kindergarten classroom and learns what he will be doing his first year of school.

General Series Books

Arthur books by Marc Brown. Little, Brown.

Berenstain Bears books by Stan and Jan Berenstain. Random House.

Clifford books by Norman Bridwell. Scholastic.

Name Tag Patterns for Count on Books

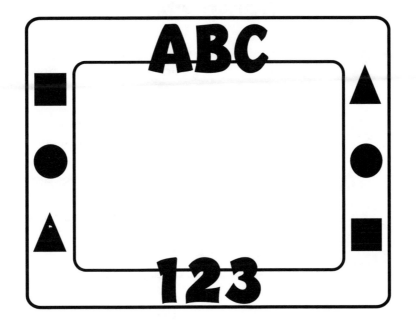

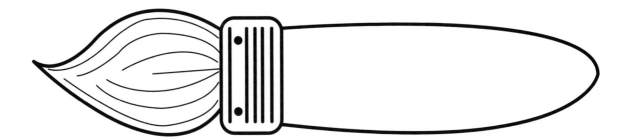

Traveling Tales
Transportation

Before Storytime

Name Tags

Copy the name tag patterns on page 69. Make enough copies so you have one nametag per child. Cut the nametags out and color them if you like. Pin the nametag to the child's shirt or punch a hole in it and string it with yarn for a necklace.

Props

- an old steering wheel to drive in—you might be able to obtain one at a junkyard relatively inexpensively

- hat with an airplane wings pin

- train whistle or engineer's cap

- nautical attire

Note: The sky's the limit with this theme so keep your eyes open at rummage sales.

Storytime

- Introduce the theme by asking the children about their name tags.

- Ask, "What kind of vehicle did you take to get there?" "How many of you have seen a big truck up close?" "Have you ever been on a boat, a bus or a plane?"

- Sing the storytime song on page 7.

- Intersperse stories, fingerplays, songs and activities that fit your theme and time frame.

Snack

Create a transportation snack using celery sticks, toothpicks, carrots and peanut butter.

Place the celery sticks ribbed-side down and slice carrots into small circles. Make wheels by securing the carrot sticks to the celery with toothpicks and spread peanut butter on the inside of the celery for cargo. Sprinkle raisins or chocolate chips on top of the peanut butter to add to the cargo's load.

Discussion Questions

Ask specific questions to reinforce comprehension concepts.

For example:

- "Do you remember what some of the things were that the train carried in the book *I Love Trains?*"

- "Did you notice where the elephant and his friends were coming out of in the book *Let's Take the Bus?*"

- "Who else was in the story *Five Little Monkeys Wash the Car?*"

- "Have you ever seen a hot air balloon like in the book *Bear On a Bike?*"

Wrapping It Up

Sing the goodbye song on page 8.

Songs

Riding in the Car

Sung to the tune: "Farmer in the Dell"

We're riding in the car.
We're riding in the car.
Heigh-ho, away we go,
We're riding in the car.

We're going oh so far.
We're going oh so far.
Heigh-ho, away we go,
We're riding in the car.

Watching the World Go By

Sung to the tune: "My Bonnie Lies Over the Ocean"

I love to ride in a car,
Now I will tell you why.
I love to look out of the window,
And watch the cars go by.

Cars, cars, cars, cars,
Just watch the cars go by, go by.
Cars, cars, cars, cars,
Just watch the cars go by.

(Add other things the children see out of a car window.)

Traffic Light Song

Sung to the tune: "Mary Had a Little Lamb"

Can you see the traffic light,
Traffic light, traffic light?
Green means GO and yellow means SLOW,
And red means STOP, STOP, STOP!

I'm a Big Truck

Sung to the tune: "Oh My Darling Clementine"

I'm a big truck,
Rolling down the road.
I'm as big as a football field.
I carry lots of things,
And I make sure,
That I handle them with care.

I drive from one place,
To another.
I go from here to there.
Sometimes bringing you ice cream,
Or even teddy bears.

Cows and chickens,
Pigs and trees,
My big truck can haul anything.
I don't want to haul bees,
But what do you think I should bring?

Train

Sung to the tune: "Row, Row, Row, Your Boat"

Ride, ride, ride the train,
Quickly down the track.
Clickety, clickety, clickety clack.
When will it be back?

Down By the Station *Traditional*

Down by the station, early in the morning,
See the little puff-puff trains all in a row.
Man in the engine pulls a little lever.
Choo-choo-whoo-whoo,
Off we go!

(Make train sounds, move arms at sides and bend elbows to symbolize train wheels.)

I've Been Working on the Railroad
Traditional

I've been workin' on the railroad,
All the live long day.
I've been workin' on the railroad,
Just to pass the time away.
Don't you hear the whistle blowing?
Rise up so early in the morn.
Don't you hear the captain shouting
Dinah, blow your horn?"

Dinah, won't you blow,
Dinah, won't you blow,
Dinah, won't you blow your horn?
Dinah, won't you blow,
Dinah, won't you blow,
Dinah, won't you blow your horn?

Someone's in the kitchen with Dinah.
Someone's in the kitchen, I know.
Someone's in the kitchen with Dinah,
Strumming on the old banjo.

Off We Go

Sung to the tune: "Frére Jacques"

Here's the train, here's the train.
All aboard, all aboard.
Chug-a chug-a choo-choo.
Chug-a chug-a choo-choo.
Off we go, off we go!

Other verses:

Here's the truck … brroom-a-brroom-a-honk-honk!

Here's the airplane … whoosh-a-whoosh-a-zoom-zoom!

Here's the bus … chug-a-chug-a-beep-beep!

Here's the boat … chug-a-chug-a-toot-toot!

I'm An Airplane

Sung to the tune: "Oh My Darling Clementine"

I'm an airplane, I'm an airplane,
(Spread arms as if airplane wings.)
Flying high up in the sky.
(Fly slowly around the room.)
Flying higher, flying higher,
(Hold arms higher as they are outstretched.)
As we watch the clouds go by.

I'm an airplane, I'm an airplane,
(Continue flying.)
See me flying all around.
Flying lower, flying lower,
(Bring arms down lower as you fly.)
Till I land down on the ground.
(Pretend to land and be seated.)

Did You Ever See an Airplane?

Sung to the tune: "Did You Ever See a Lassie?"

Did you ever see an airplane,
An airplane, an airplane?
Did you ever see an airplane,
Way up in the sky?

There are big ones and small ones,
And short ones and tall ones.
Did you ever see an airplane
Way up in the sky?

The Bus Song

Sung to the tune: "Pop Goes the Weasel"

I drive the bus around the town,
I stop at every corner.
My blinking lights and brakes go on,
Swish goes the door.

A dollar for a ride around town,
A quarter for a transfer.
Put your money in the slot,
Swish goes the door.

Row, Row, Row Your Boat *Traditional*

Row, row, row, your boat,
Gently down the stream.
Merrily, merrily, merrily, merrily,
Life is but a dream!

Rub a Dub Dub *Traditional*

Rub a dub dub.
Three men in a tub.
And who do you think they be?
The butcher, the baker,
The candlestick maker,
All rowing their way out to sea.

Whoosh! Goes the Car Wash

Sung to the tune: "Pop Goes the Weasel"

We're waiting at the car wash,
It seems to take forever.
Our car is full of dirt and mud,
One more car ready.

We wait in line.
I wish it would,
Go a little faster.
Now it's finally our turn,
Whoosh! Goes the water.

We splish and splash,
In soapy suds,
It rinses us with water.
Now it's time to get the wax,
Whoosh! Goes more water.

We're all washed now it's time to go,
We pull up really slow.
We hear the dryer start to blow,
Whoosh! Now we're drying.

We creep and creep,
On through the stall.
We're almost all dry now.
Oops! The dryer just turned off,
Whoosh! We're all clean … WOW!

Fingerplays

Riding in My Van

I have on my vest and my visor too!
(Touch chest/hold hand over eyes.)
They are new and the color is blue!
(Clap on "new" and "blue.")
I'm riding in my van and taking in the view.
(Pretend to drive—look around.)
Maybe next time you can come too!
(Point to children and continue driving.)

Car Ride

To go near or to go far,
(Pretend to drive.)
You can ride inside a car.
Give your seat belt a good click,
(Pretend to fasten seat belt.)
Now that ought to do the trick.
It's good to know you're safe and sound,
(Hug self.)
When you're driving around the town.

Driving Down the Street

Let's drive our car down the street,
(Pretend to drive the car.)
Always looking straight ahead.
(Point straight.)
We'll have to stop when the light turns red.
(Put hand up, palm out to indicate stop.)
Waiting and watching through the wind-
shield clean,
(Move hands like wipers.)
Now we can go,
(Pretend to drive.)
The light turned green.

When I Get Into the Car

When I get into the car,
I buckle up for near or far.
It holds me in my seat so tight.
I feel safe I know it's right.
I use my seat belt every day,
So I'll be safe in every way.

Windshield Wiper

I'm a windshield wiper.
(Bend arm with fingers pointing up.)
This is how I go.
(Move arm left to right, pivoting at the elbow.)
Back and forth, back and forth,
(Continue back and forth motion.)
In the rain and snow.

The Freight Train

Clickety clack, clickety clack,
The train speeds over the railroad track.
It rolls and rattles and screeches its song,
And pulls and jiggles its freight along.

Clickety clack, clickety clack!
The engine in front it's big and it's black.
The cars are filled with lots of things,
Like milk or oil or mattress springs.

Clickety clack, clickety clack!
The engineer waves and I wave back.
I count the cars as the freight train goes,
And the whistle blows and blows and blows!

Choo-Choo Train

This is a choo-choo train.
(Bend arms at elbows.)
Puffing down the track.
(Rotate arms in forward motion.)
Now it's going forward.
Now it's going back.
(Rotate arms in backward motion.)

Now the bell is ringing.
(Pull bell cord.)
Now the whistle blows.
(Make train sound.)
What a lot of noise it makes,
(Cover ears with hands.)
Everywhere it goes.
(Stretch out arms.)

My Tiny Train

My tiny train,
(Indicate a row of short cars.)
Rolls round and round.
(Move hands in a circle.)

It runs through tunnels,
(Thumb and forefinger form tunnel, other hand passes through.)
In the ground.
It even climbs up mountainsides,
("Train" hand passes over an upright hand.)
While a whistle blows,
(Hand pretends to pull whistle cord.)
As it rides and rides.
WHOO! WHOO! WHOO!
(Make train whistle sound.)

Activities

Car Wash

Read *Five Little Monkeys Wash the Car* by Eileen Christelow or *Car Wash* by Sandra and Susan Steen. Then, send cars through the car wash.

Supplies needed:

- crayons
- paper
- cinnamon
- water in a spray bottle

Directions:

1. Copy the car pattern on page 69. Enlarge if necessary. Make one car for each child.

2. Have the children color the car with crayons.

3. Have the children sprinkle some cinnamon on the car to get the car "muddy."

4. Use a spray bottle to have the children "wash" the car with misted water. To speed the drying process the children may blow on the car like the blowers in a car wash.

Gross Motor Skills Activity

Play a version of the "freeze game." When you say "green" the children move around the room as any mode of transportation (remind them that just like with real vehicles they must proceed with caution and be careful not to run into other vehicles). When you say "red" the children must stop and turn off all engines, get off their bikes, etc. You may wish to name some of the children and the mode of transportation they are using. Ask them to think up a new vehicle and repeat the game. If you prefer a more organized version, have the children name a type of transportation and when the light turns "green," everyone drives that type of vehicle. You may wish to ask them to all stay on the road, the runway, etc. Everyone stops when the light turns "red."

Trucks

Read *Truck Jam* by Paul Strickland, *Truck* by Donald Crews or *Joshua James Likes Trucks* by Catherine Petrie.

Supplies needed:

- construction paper
- glue
- scissors
- cardboard
- crayons or markers

Directions:

1. Cut out assorted shapes or make tracers out of stiff cardboard so the children can cut them out.

2. Have the children assemble a truck from a triangle, square, circles and a rectangle. A square makes a good truck cab, a rectangle looks like the trailer end of a big truck and circles may be added for wheels. Various sized squares and rectangles can be added for windows and smoke stacks.

3. Glue the truck to a background piece of paper.

4. Use crayons or markers to add details to the trucks.

Gross Motor Skills Activity

Read *I Love Trains* by Philemon Sturges, *Planes* by Anne Rockwell, *First Flight* by David McPhail or *Boats For Bedtime* by Olga Litowinsky.

Line up chairs in a row so everyone has a seat. Pretend the chairs are cars on a train or seats on a plane or an ocean liner. Everyone follows the leader (the child in the first chair) and does what the person in front of them is doing, e.g., sounding the horn on the boat, rolling down the railroad tracks, buckling up and flying high or landing after a long plane trip. Discuss conventional ways as well as silly modes of transportation. Have they ever thought of a different way to get from place to place, such as an ice cream mobile? Not just a truck that sells or delivers ice cream, but one made from ice cream cones and ice cream! Maybe even made from ice! Ask how that kind of vehicle would move and how far you would be able to drive it. What kind of wheels would it have? etc.

Math Activity

Lay sheets of paper down on the floor (you may use different colors to help distinguish lanes) and have the children predict how far they think their car or truck will go (use Matchbox cars and trucks). Mark their prediction. Remind them their car or truck must stay in its lane. Count out the distance by the pieces of paper each one has traveled. Whose vehicle traveled the farthest? Who was closest to their prediction?

Fine Motor Skills Activity

Place cornmeal in one rectangular-shaped plastic tub and water in another. Have toy boats, cars, trucks and trains available to play with in the tubs. Place a towel under each of the tubs for easier clean up.

Storytime Books to Share

Barney's Book of Trains by Linda Cress Dowdy. Lyrick Pub., 1998. Barney and B. J. go on a train ride and show various types of trains.

Bear On a Bike by Stella Blackstone. Barefoot Books, 2001. Learn about different modes of transportation with a big friendly bear as he travels by bicycle, raft and even hot air balloon.

Big Truck and Little Truck by Jan Carr. Scholastic, 2000. Big Truck and Little Truck work together on Farley's Farm until the day that Big Truck is towed away for repairs and Little Truck must haul produce to the city all by himself.

Boats For Bedtime by Olga Litowinsky. Houghton Mifflin, 1999. A child imagines all kinds of boats in all kinds of places as he settles down to sleep.

Car Wash by Sandra and Susan Steen. Penguin USA, 2001. While sitting inside their car, two children enjoy the soapy sights and watery sounds of the car wash.

Clifford Takes a Trip by Norman Bridwell. Scholastic, 1985. Clifford gets lonely when Emily Elizabeth and her family go on vacation, so he sets out after them.

Curious George Rides a Bike by H. A. Rey. Houghton Mifflin, 1973. George the monkey gets a bike from his friend and goes on adventures.

Ferryboat by Betsy and Giulio Maestro. Crowell, 1986. A family crosses a river on a ferryboat and observes how a ferry operates.

First Flight by David McPhail. Little, Brown, 1991. A boy's teddy bear becomes life size on this first airplane trip.

Five Little Monkeys Wash the Car by Eileen Christelow. Clarion, 2000. Five little monkeys wash the family car before trying to sell it, but that's only the beginning of their adventures with the old heap.

The Flying School Bus by Seymour Reit. Golden Books, 1990. The school bus was old, its fenders were bent, but before the old school bus could be hauled off to the junkyard, it flies off.

Harbor by Donald Crews. Greenwillow Books, 1982. Presents various kinds of boats, which come and go in a busy harbor.

How Will We Get to the Beach? by Brigitte Luciani. North-South Books, 2003. Roxanne decides to go to the beach, but with so much to carry how will she get there?

If I Had a Snowplow by Jean L. Patrick. Boyds Mills Press, 2001. Each month, a little boy imagines what nice things he could do for his mother if he had a real snow plow, tree spade, bulldozer or other machine.

I Love Trains by Philemon Sturges. HarperCollins, 2001. A boy expresses his love of trains, describing the many kinds of train cars and their special jobs.

Joshua James Likes Trucks by Catherine Petrie. Scholastic, 2000. Joshua James likes all kinds of trucks—big trucks, little trucks, trucks that go up and trucks that go down.

Let's Take the Bus by Chris Economos. Steck-Vaughn, 1989. Five foolish animal friends have trouble getting home on the bus.

The Little Engine That Could retold by Watty Piper. Putnam, 1990. When the other engines refuse, the Little Blue Engine tries to pull a stranded train full of toys and good food over the mountain.

The Little Engine That Could Helps Out retold by Watty Piper. Platt & Munk, 1999. The Little Blue Engine helps a clown in a circus ride a bike. Told in rebus format.

Mr. Gumpy's Motor Car by John Burningham. Puffin Books, 1977. Mr. Gumpy's human and animal friends squash into his old car and go for a drive—until it starts to rain.

Muppet Babies On the Go by Emily Paul. Grolier, 1992. The Muppet Babies show how to get from here to there riding bicycles, trains, a rocket ship and even a hot-air balloon.

My Sister's Rusty Bike by Jim Aylesworth. Atheneum Books, 1996. A rhyming tale of a zany, zigzag trip around America.

The New Bike by Marie Vinje. School Zone Publishing Co., 1993. Lee gets a new bike and learns to ride.

Planes by Anne Rockwell. Penguin Putnam, 1991. Simple text and illustrations introduce different types of airplanes.

Red Racer by Audrey Wood. Simon & Schuster, 1999. Nona tries desperately to get rid of her junky old bike so that she can get the Deluxe Red Racer which she sees in the store window.

Round Trip by Ann Jonas. William Morrow & Co., 1991. Black and white illustrations record the sights on a day trip to the city and back home again to the country.

School Bus by Donald Crews. HarperCollins, 2002. Follows the progress of the school buses as they take children to school and bring them home again.

Shortcut by Donald Crews. William Morrow & Co., 1996. Children taking a shortcut along a railroad track find excitement and danger when the train approaches.

Things That Go by Anne Rockwell. Penguin Putnam, 1991. Pictures naming many things that go in a park, in the city, on the water, etc.

Train Song by Diane Siebert. HarperCollins, 1993. Rhymed text and illustrations describe the journey of transcontinental trains.

Truck by Donald Crews. HarperCollins, 1997. Follows the journey of a truck from loading to unloading.

Truck Jam by Paul Strickland. Ragged Bears, 2000. Pop-up pictures depict several trucks engaged in various activities such as pouring sand, getting stuck in traffic and being towed.

Name Tag Patterns for Traveling Tales

Books, the Greatest Present

Un-birthdays and Presents

Before Storytime

Name Tags

Copy the name tag patterns on page 74. Make enough copies so you have one name-tag per child. Cut the name tags out and color them if you like. Pin the name tag to the child's shirt or punch a hole in it and string it with yarn for a necklace.

Props

- wear a big bow around your neck to indicate a present
- have a box wrapped with a surprise inside for all (e.g., stickers, candy, bookmarks or a special stamper and stamp pad to give each child a stamp on their hand)

Storytime

- Introduce the theme by asking the children about their name tags.
- Explain that we have one day that is our special birthday, but so many other days that we can celebrate. We call these our un-birthdays!
- Sing the storytime song on page 7.
- Intersperse stories, fingerplays, songs and activities that fit your theme and time frame.

Snack

Serve cupcakes or birthday cake. Sing "Happy Birthday."

Discussion Questions

Ask specific questions to reinforce comprehension concepts.

For example:

- "Would you like to get a bone for your birthday like Biscuit did in the book *Happy Birthday, Biscuit!*?" "Why or why not?"
- "Did you like moving the wrapping paper to the beat during the story *Wrapping Paper Romp*?"

Wrapping It Up

Sing the goodbye song on page 8.

Songs

Happy Birthday

Happy birthday to us.
Happy birthday to us.
It's all our un-birthday's
Today's a special day!

Your Un-Birthday

Sung to the tune: "If You're Happy and You Know It"

If today is your un-birthday clap your hands. *(Clap, clap.)*
If today is your un-birthday clap your hands. *(Clap, clap.)*
It might not be the real day,
But we'll make it special anyway.

We'll say it's your un-birthday and yell hooray!
Hooray!

Today is the Birthday

Sung to the tune: "On Top of Old Smokey"

Today is the birthday of somebody who,
Is happy and smiling and right in this room.
So look all around you and tell me just who,
Is happy and smiling?
My goodness it's you!

Birthday Fun

Sung to the tune: "Row, Row, Row Your Boat"

Hurrah, hurrah, hurrah, it's grand,
Today's your un-birthday.
We'll have a special time today,
With books and games to play.

A Reason to Celebrate

Sung to the tune: "Twinkle, Twinkle, Little Star"

It's our un-birthday today.
We'll make it great in every way.
We're celebrating that we're all special,
Happy un-birthday today!

Zippity Dooh Dah

Zippity dooh dah, zippity ay,
My oh my what a wonderful day.
Plenty of sunshine coming your way,
Zippity dooh dah it's our un-birthday!

We can play that it's our birthday.
We can pretend it's actual,
Even though we know what's factual.

Zippity dooh dah, zippity ay,
Let's have a fun pretend birthday!

Fingerplay and Poem

Celebrate!

Let's make a cake,
(Pretend to mix a cake.)
To celebrate for you.
(Point to children.)
How happy we are that you are you.
(Smile and point to children.)

We don't have to wait for your real birthday,
(Shake head.)
Cause everyday is a special day!
(Spread arms out wide.)
Let's celebrate we're all here,
With the best present we can give all year.
(Hug self.)
A smile for a friend
(Place fingers near lips and smile.)
Hoping their happiness never ends.
(Spread arms out wide.)

Presents

This poem works well as the end of program wrap up. It could also be used to pass out a surprise for the children.

Here is a present just for you.
Everything wrapped so you have no clue,
What's inside the pretty box.
Could it be a pair of socks?
How about a cute toy bear?
Maybe you say … you don't care,
As long as it's a present for you.
But how do we show we care, too?
A thank you, a hug, a smile would do,
Showing you love someone is important, too.
Getting presents is really neat,
But giving is also a real treat!

Activities

Gift Boxes

Read *Happy Birthday, Moon* by Frank Asch or *Happy Birthday, Biscuit!* by Alyssa Satin Capucilli. Then decorate gift boxes with the children.

Supplies needed:

- collapsible gift boxes (try asking for them at candy and floral shops)

- crayons or markers

- scrap material

- beads, sequins, ribbon, old greeting cards

- glue

Directions:

1. Have the children decorate gift boxes with markers or crayons, scrap materials, old birthday cards, beads, etc.

2. Use the box for a homemade present or keep it as a trinket box for secret treasures.

Present, Present Who's Got the Present? (Gross Motor Skills)

This game is played like "Doggie, Doggie where's your bone?" All of the children sit in a circle. One child is the "birthday person" who sits in the middle of the circle. The child in the middle covers his or her eyes while one child hides a small wrapped box. All of the children should look as if they are hiding the box. Then the birthday person opens his or her eyes and chooses the child hiding the box. If correct, the child hiding the box now becomes the "birthday person." If incorrect, the child hiding the box shows it and then becomes the "birthday person."

Bake a Birthday Cake

Mix together a cake mix using the directions on the box. Discuss the ingredients, counting and measuring. Allow each child a turn at mixing the batter. Discuss the cause and effect of making the cake, as well as opposites such as dry vs. wet, liquid vs. solid and cold vs. hot.

Birthday Art

Supplies needed:

- crayons or markers
- cake decorations
- glue
- colored plastic wrap
- ribbon
- sequins
- birthday cake, cupcakes or sugar cookies
- frosting tubes

Birthday Cake: Enlarge the birthday cake and candle patterns on page 74. Have the children add the correct number of candles for their age. Children may color their cakes with crayons and markers or glue on cake decorations (sprinkles, red hot candies, stars, etc.) Offer colored plastic wrap to glue on for the candle's flame.

Birthday Presents: Use the present pattern on page 74 and enlarge if necessary. Have the children decorate it with ribbon scraps or sequins, then color it in.

Edible Art: You can also make edible art. Have the children decorate a birthday cupcake, piece of cake or sugar cookie with frosting tubes and cake decorations.

Fine Motor Skills Activity

Count and sort birthday candles according to color, size and shape.

Note: This activity works well before the program as the children come in or after the program as they wait for their caregiver to pick them up.

Pin the Candle on the Cake

Enlarge the birthday cake and candle patterns on page 74. Color them if you wish. Hang the cake at a level the children can reach. Blindfold the children, then have them stick the candles to the cake using double stick tape.

Storytime Books to Share

Arthur's Birthday by Marc Brown. Little, Brown, 1991. Their friends must decide which party to attend when Francine schedules her birthday party for the same day as Arthur's birthday party.

Benjamin's 365 Birthdays by Judi Barrett. Atheneum, 1992. Benjamin figures out how to have a birthday every day of the year.

Bunny Money by Rosemary Wells. Dial Books for Young Readers, 1997. Max and Ruby spend so much on emergencies while shopping for Grandma's birthday present that they just barely have enough money left for gifts.

Bunny Party by Rosemary Wells. Viking, 2001. Max and his big sister Ruby disagree about which of their toys to invite to Grandma's birthday party.

Clifford's Birthday Party by Norman Bridwell. Scholastic, 1988. It's Clifford's birthday and Emily Elizabeth is throwing a big party. There's a piñata to break, presents to open and a very special birthday cake. Surprise! Out pops Clifford's whole family to help celebrate.

Elephant Small Goes to a Party by Sally Grindley. Little Barron's, 1999. Elephant Small has lots of fun at Jolly Dog's birthday party. All the animals have tasty things to eat and drink and enjoy playing party games.

A Gift by Claudia Fregosi. Prentice-Hall International, 1976. Wanting to express his love for his wife, a man finally finds a way to combine all of the things that she loves the most into one gift.

Happy Birthday, Biscuit! by Alyssa Satin Capucilli. HarperCollins, 1999. Biscuit celebrates his first birthday with his cat and dog friends.

Happy Birthday, Dear Duck by Eve Bunting. Clarion, 1988. Duck's birthday gifts from his animal friends are wonderful but cannot be used away from the water, a problem eventually solved by the arrival of his last gift.

Happy Birthday, Jesse Bear! by Nancy White Carlstrom. Simon and Schuster, 1994. Jessie Bear prepares for his birthday party with his family and friends.

Happy Birthday, Moon by Frank Asch. Aladdin Books, 2000. Bear loves the moon so much he wants to give him a birthday present.

Ice-Cold Birthday by Maryann Cocca-Leffler. Putnam, 1992. A big snowstorm threatens to spoil a birthday party but also creates some unforeseen opportunities for special fun.

It's My Birthday Too! by Lynne Jonell. Putnam, 2001. Christopher would rather have a dog than a little brother who ruins his birthday parties, but when his brother begins to act like a puppy, Christopher has a change of heart.

Max's Birthday by Rosemary Wells. Dial Books for Young Readers, 1998. Max's sister Ruby gives him a wind-up lobster for his birthday.

One Bad Thing About Birthdays by David R. Collin. Harcourt Brace, 1981. A boy tries to decide what to wish for on his birthday.

Something Special For Me by Vera B. Williams. William Morrow & Co., 1986. Rosa has difficulty choosing a special birthday present to buy with the coins her mother and grandmother have saved, until she hears a man playing beautiful music on the accordion.

A Surprise for Max by Hanne Türk. Neugebauer Press, 1982. A wordless picture book of Max the mouse finding a present.

Wrapping Paper Romp by Patricia Hubbell. HarperCollins, 1998. A playful poem exploring the simple fun of opening a present. This is a fun story to tell to a rap beat. Have the children tap out the beat as you tell the story. Give each child a piece of tissue paper so they can act out the story.

Name Tag Patterns for Books, the Greatest Present

Cooking Up Good Stories

Food and Cookies

Before Storytime

Name Tags

Copy the name tag patterns on page 80. Make enough copies so you have one name tag per child. Cut the name tags out and color them if you like. Pin the name tag to the child's shirt or punch a hole in it and string it with yarn for a necklace.

Props

- apron and chef's hat (check with local restaurants)
- big cooking pot for your stories
- various kitchen utensils
- play food for your cooking pot
- make sandwiches out of two pieces of foam cut in a bread shape with felt between them to make meat, lettuce, etc.

Storytime

- Introduce the theme by asking the children about their name tags.
- Ask the children if they know what the kitchen tools are and how they are used. Have the children name the food in your cooking pot.
- Sing the storytime song on page 7.
- Intersperse stories, fingerplays, songs and activities that fit your theme and time frame.

Snack

If you chose to cook during the program, serve your creation with options the children might not be accustomed to such as jam, honey, peanut butter, marshmallow fluff, apple butter, flavored syrups, etc. These options allow the children to look at things differently and be open to new experiences.

Discussion Questions

Ask specific questions to reinforce comprehension concepts.

For example:

- "Would you like to get your food dropped from the sky as in *Cloudy With a Chance of Meatballs*?"
- "Would you give a moose a muffin if he came to your house like in the story *If You Give a Moose a Muffin*?"

Wrapping It Up

Sing the goodbye song on page 8.

Songs

Dippy Doughnut Song

Sung to the tune: "Baa Baa Black Sheep"

Yum, yum doughnuts,
Chocolate iced,
Glazed and twisted,
Warm and nice.

Cream filled with peanuts on top.
Long johns! Jelly!
I can't stop!

Better than a sticky roll,
Eat them right down to the hole!

Pease Porridge Hot *Traditional*

Pease porridge hot!
Pease porridge cold!
Pease porridge in the pot
Nine days old.

Some like it hot,
Some like it cold,
Some like it in the pot,
Nine days old.

On Top of Spaghetti *Traditional*

On top of spaghetti,
All covered with cheese,
I lost my poor meatball,
When somebody sneezed.

It rolled off the table,
And on to the floor,
And then my poor meatball,
Rolled out of the door.

It rolled in the garden,
And under a bush,
And then my poor meatball,
Was nothing but mush.

Muffin Man *Traditional*

Oh, do you know the muffin man,
The muffin man, the muffin man.
Oh, do you know the muffin man,
That lives on Drury Lane?

Oh, yes, I know the muffin man,
The muffin man, the muffin man.
Oh, yes, I know the muffin man,
That lives on Drury Lane.

Fingerplays

I Know a Treat

I know a treat that has a hole,
(Put fingers together to form a circle.)
As you can plainly see.
(Place fingers by your eyes.)
Doughnut, doughnut, doughnut.
Save a bite for me!
(Point to self.)

I know a treat that has a hole,
(Place fingers together to form a circle.)
But where could it be?
(Place hands out palms up, shrug.)
Yummy, yummy, yum.
(Rub tummy.)
Now only the hole is left, can you see?
(Place fingers together in a circle; put other finger through the hole.)

Five Little Cookies

Five little cookies with frosting galore,
(Hold up the correct number of fingers.)
Mother ate the pink one and then there were four.

Four little cookies, two and two you see,
Father ate the green one, then there were three.

Three little cookies, but before I knew,
Sister ate the yellow one, then there were two.

Two little cookies, oh, what fun!
Brother ate the brown one, then there was one.

One little cookie, watch me run!
I ate the red one, then there were none!

The Chef

I really love to cook.
(Point to self.)
I am a chef you see.
(Point to hat.)
I chop and cook and bake,

Until around three.
(*Pretend to chop … hold up three fingers.*)

Mixing, pouring, rolling,
(*Pretend to mix, pour, roll.*)
Soups, potatoes, rolls,
Veggies, fruits, meats and even doughnut holes!
(*Rub tummy.*)

Working to make foods,
That are good for you and for me.
(*Point to children and self.*)
Take a taste and you will see!
(*Pretend to offer taste.*)

Five Little Hot Dogs

Five little hot dogs frying in the pan.
(*Hold up five fingers.*)
The grease got hot and one went … BAM!
(*Say loudly and clap.*)

Four little hot dogs (etc.)
(*Hold up appropriate number of fingers.*)

Repeat verses for three and two.

One little hot dog frying in the pan.
(*Hold up one finger.*)
The grease got hot and it went … BAM!
(*Say loudly and clap.*)

No little hot dogs frying in the pan.
(*Show zero with your fingers.*)
The grease got hot and the pan went … BAM!
(*Say loudly and clap!*)

Activities

Gross Motor Skills Activity

Have a relay race with plastic fruits and vegetables or cards of the same. Place a large empty cooking pot at one end and have the children form two teams. Hand each child a fruit or vegetable as their turn comes up. Whichever team "cooks" their soup first (gets the pictures or pieces to the pot) needs to name all the fruits and vegetables in the pot.

Cookie Decorating

Read *The Doorbell Rang* by Pat Hutchins or *The Best Mouse Cookie* by Laura Joffe Numeroff. Then have cookies ready for the children to decorate as edible art.

Supplies needed:

- cookies
- white frosting
- food coloring
- plastic knives or craft sticks
- cake decorations (*optional*)

Note: Requires prior preparation of cookies.

Directions:

1. Have the children mix different colors of frosting. Discuss how red and blue make purple, yellow and blue make green, etc.
2. Frost the cookies and add decorations.

Spaghetti

Read *Wednesday is Spaghetti Day* by Maryann Cocca-Leffler, *Daddy Makes the Best Spaghetti* by Anna Grossnickle Hines or *Cloudy with a Chance of Meatballs* by Judi Barrett.

Supplies needed:

- glue
- yarn (white or cream)
- small paper plates
- red paint
- brown tissue paper

Directions:

1. Have the children glue white or cream colored yarn to a small paper plate.
2. Paint on the "sauce" with red paint.
3. Crumple brown tissue paper into small bits for the "meatballs." Glue them onto the "spaghetti."

Doughnuts

Read *Banana Moon* by Janet Perry Marshall, *Walter the Baker* by Eric Carle or *Uncle's Bakery* by Dana Meachen Rau.

Supplies needed:

- cardboard
- crayons or markers
- glue
- cake decorations

Directions:

1. Cut out doughnut shapes from card-board.

2. Have the children decorate them with crayons or markers. Glue on cake decorations.

Easy Corn Bread

Make the corn bread and discuss basic math and science skills, measurements, cause and effect and opposites such as wet and dry, liquid and solid and cold and hot.

Ingredients:

- 1¼ cups flour
- ¾ cup corn meal
- ¼ cup sugar
- 2 tsps. baking powder
- ½ tsp. salt *(optional)*
- 1 cup milk
- ¼ cup vegetable oil
- 1 beaten egg

Directions:

1. Grease an 8 or 9 inch pan and preheat oven to 400°F.

2. Combine the dry ingredients.

3. Mix together milk, egg and oil.

4. Add the dry ingredients to the wet ingredients. Mix until moistened. Pour into a pan and bake for 20–25 minutes or until a light golden brown. A toothpick inserted in the center should come out clean.

Painting

Supplies needed:

- paint
- corn starch

- baster
- pastry brush
- vegetables
- cooked spaghetti noodles

Directions:

- Have the children use turkey basters or pastry brushes to paint pictures of fruits and vegetables.

- Have the children use various vegetables such as potatoes, carrots, beans, peas, etc., to stamp paper.

- Have the children paint with cooked spaghetti noodles.

Note: Add cornstarch to the paint to help it dry faster.

Fine Motor Skills Activity

Have the children sort play food or cards with pictures of various foods. They can sort the foods according to color and type.

Circle Time Game

Play "I'm thinking of something." Describe how a food tastes or looks. Give a clue in the beginning with the type of food such as, "I'm thinking of a fruit that is red and crunchy, sweet and you don't eat the seeds" (apple). Or "I'm thinking of something you usually have after dinner, it's sweet and round, and has brown chips in it. It's baked in the oven and is usually crunchy" (a chocolate chip cookie).

Storytime Books to Share

Banana Moon by Janet Perry Marshall. Greenwillow Books, 1998. Die-cut illustrations of various edible treats are transformed into sunsets, clouds, turtles, fish and other sights seen while sailing on the sea.

The Best Mouse Cookie by Laura Joffe Numeroff. Laura Geringer Books, 1999. The mouse from *If You Give a Mouse a Cookie* bakes in his own little mouse house.

Cloudy with a Chance of Meatballs by Judi Barrett. Aladdin Books, 1982. In Chewandswallow, meals rain from the sky at appropriate times of the day, but a change in weather blows in massive problems.

Daddy Makes the Best Spaghetti by Anna Grossnickle Hines. Trumpet Club, 1992. Not only does Corey's father make the best spaghetti, but he also dresses up as Bathman and acts like a barking dog.

The Doorbell Rang by Pat Hutchins. Scholastic, 1986. Each time the doorbell rings, there are more people who have come to share Ma's wonderful cookies.

D. W. the Picky Eater by Marc Brown. Little, Brown, 1995. Because her eating habits cause some problems, Arthur the aardvark's younger sister has to stay home when her family eats out.

Gregory, the Terrible Eater by Mitchell Sharmat. Four Winds Press, 1980. Gregory wants orange juice and eggs for breakfast. His parents are terribly upset! Why can't Gregory eat striped ties and violins like the rest of the goats?

Hedgehog Bakes a Cake by Maryann Macdonald. Gareth Stevens Pub., 1996. As hedgehog starts to make a cake, his friends stop by one by one and each has advice for the project. Includes a cake recipe.

If You Give a Moose a Muffin by Laura Joffe Numeroff. HarperCollins, 1994. If a big hungry moose comes to visit, you might want to give him a muffin to make him feel at home. But then he'll ask for jam and more muffins; a circular tale with silly illustrations.

If You Give a Mouse a Cookie by Laura Joffe Numeroff. Scholastic, 1989. This circle story relates the cycle of requests a mouse is likely to make after you give him a cookie.

If You Give a Pig a Pancake by Laura Joffe Numeroff. Laura Geringer Books, 2000. One thing leads to another when you give a pig a pancake.

Maisy Makes Gingerbread by Lucy Cousins. Candlewick Press, 1999. Maisy the mouse makes gingerbread cookies and shares them with her friends Charley and Tallulah.

Mouse Mess by Linea Aplind Riley. Blue Sky Press, 1997. When a mouse ventures out for a nighttime snack, it turns into a midnight mess.

Mr. Cookie Baker by Monica Wellington. Puffin Books, 1992. After a day of making and selling cookies, Mr. Baker gets to enjoy one himself.

Pancakes, Pancakes by Eric Carle. Scholastic, 1992. Before Jack can eat his longed-for pancake breakfast, he must cut the wheat to grind for flour, gather the eggs, milk the cow, churn the butter and build a fire.

Today is Monday by Eric Carle. Philomel Books, 2001. Monday begins with string beans and Tuesday is spaghetti day. Different animals eat their way through the days of the week, teaching the names of the days as they go.

Two for Stew by Laura Numeroff and Barney Saltzberg. Simon & Schuster, 1996. Because the restaurant has no more stew and the grandmother who makes it is out for the evening, two friends find a different way to enjoy themselves.

Uncle's Bakery by Dana Meachen Rau. Compass Point Books, 2002. A young girl visits her uncle's bakery with her mother and together they use all their senses to enjoy the visit.

Walter the Baker by Eric Carle. Simon & Schuster, 1995. Walter the Baker is famous for his breads, rolls, cookies, tarts and pies. The Duke and Duchess love his warm sweet rolls, but when the cat spills the milk, Walter puts water in the dough instead. He gets very creative while trying to save his job.

Wednesday is Spaghetti Day by Maryann Cocca-Leffler. Scholastic, 1990. Ever wonder what your cat does at home when you're out? Catrina the cat invites her friends over for a delicious spaghetti lunch every Wednesday.

Other Media to Share

Madeline at Cooking School. Golden Book Video, 1993. 30 minutes. Madeline and her friends learn the most important ingredient in any recipe is kindness.

Name Tag Patterns for Cooking Up Good Stories

Growing Great Books
Gardens, Gardening and Vegetables

Before Storytime

Name Tags

Copy the name tag patterns on page 87. Make enough copies so you have one name-tag per child. Cut the name tags out and color them if you like. Pin the name tag to the child's shirt or punch a hole in it and string it with yarn for a necklace.

Props

- big floppy straw hat
- basket of child's plastic garden tools and plastic vegetables

Note: You might want to invite a local gardener or worker from a nursery to share what they do in their gardens and at the nursery. Have them bring some of the tools they use for show and tell.

Storytime

- Introduce the theme by asking the children about their name tags.
- Ask, "What am I carrying?" "How would you use these tools?" "Have you ever had a garden?" "What kinds of things did you plant?"
- Sing the storytime song on page 7.
- Intersperse stories, fingerplays, songs and activities that fit your theme and time frame.

Snack

Serve different fruits and vegetables with dip.

Discussion Questions

Ask specific questions to reinforce comprehension concepts.

For example:

- "We already had the date June 29, 1999. Did you hear if it really happened like in the story? Do you think it could?"

Wrapping It Up

Sing the goodbye song on page 8.

Songs

Shovels, Rakes and Even Hoes

Sung to the tune: "Twinkle, Twinkle, Little Star"

Shovels, rakes and even hoes,
Help the gardeners as *(she or he)* sows.
First *(she or he)* digs into the ground,
Then *(she or he)* plants some seeds around.

Shovels, rakes and even hoes,
Help the gardener as *(she or he)* sows.

Planting Time

Sung to the tune: "Row, Row, Row Your Boat"

Dig, dig, dig the earth,
(Make digging motion.)
Then you plant your seeds.
(Pretend to drop seeds in ground.)

A gentle rain,
(Flutter fingers.)
And bright sunshine,
(Circle arms above head.)

Will help your flowers grow.
(Hold one arm parallel to the ground and move the other arm behind it with fingers extended to represent a flower growing.)

The Seed Grows

Sung to the tune: "The Farmer In the Dell"

The gardener plants the seeds,
The gardener plants the seeds,
Deep down inside the ground,
The gardener plants the seeds.

The rain clouds give them water,
The rain clouds give them water,
Seeds need some water to drink,
The rain clouds give them water.

The sun gives heat and light,
The sun gives heat and light,
Seeds like it warm and bright,
The sun gives heat and light.

The gardener pulls the weeds,
The gardener pulls the weeds,
The seeds need the room to grow,
The gardener pulls the weeds.

The seeds grow into flowers,
The seeds grow into flowers,
Flowers that are beautiful,
The seeds grow into flowers.

Veggies

Sung to the tune: "Twinkle, Twinkle, Little Star"

Veggies, veggies, I like these,
Carrots, squash and even peas.
Potatoes, beans and corn so good,
Do you eat veggies?
Well, you should.

Give me veggies all day, please.
I'll eat them all,
Well … not lima beans!

I'm a Little Sunflower

Sung to the tune: "I'm a Little Teapot"

I'm a little sunflower,
(Sit cross-legged on the floor.)

I'm so small,
Soil, sun and water,
(On the word soil, pat the floor; on the word sun, round your arms overhead; on the word water, wiggle fingers and pretend to sprinkle the soil.)
Make me tall.
(Sit on knees.)

When I get all grown-up,
(Stand with hands on hips.)
You will see,
(Point to others.)
That I'm as big as big can be!
(Stand tall with arms overhead.)

Fingerplays

My Garden

This is my garden.
(Extend hands out.)
I rake it with care.
(Pretend to rake.)
Add some flower seeds,
(Pretend to add seeds to the ground.)
I'll plant them right there.
(Point to the ground.)

The sun will shine,
(Make a sun with your hands.)
And the rain will fall,
(Flutter fingers down.)
And my garden will blossom,
(Bring your hands up from the ground and form a flower, stand straight and tall.)
And grow straight and tall.

Five Little Peas

Five little peas in a pea pod pressed.
(Clench fingers in one hand.)
One grew, two grew and so did the rest.
(Raise fingers slowly.)
They grew and grew and did not stop,
(Stretch fingers wide.)
Until one day the pod went POP!
(Clap loudly on pop.)

My Garden

My garden has green beans,
(Hands waist high and fingers pointing down.)
Tomatoes so round,
(Form a circle with hands.)
Corn reaches high,
(Reach high.)
Carrots grown underground.
(Pat floor.)

I've watered and watered,
(Pretend to water.)
And picked all the weeds.
(Reach fingers to floor.)
Tonight we'll eat supper that
(Rub stomach.)
I planted as seeds!
(Point to self proudly.)

Digging in My Garden

I dig, dig, dig,
(Make digging motion.)
And plant some seeds.
(Poke finger between fingers of other hand.)
I rake, rake, rake,
(Make raking motion.)
And pull some weeds.
(Pull upward with fingers from palm of hand.)

I wait and watch.
(Put hands on hips.)
And soon I know,
(Point to head.)
My garden will sprout,
(Hands low, palms down.)
And start to grow!
(Raise hands toward ceiling.)

Relaxing Flowers

Five pretty sunflowers
(Hold up five fingers.)
Are standing in the sun.
(Make a circle in the air for a sun.)
Now their heads are nodding,
(Bend fingers down.)
And bowing one by one.
(Bend fingers down one at a time.)

Down, down, down, down,
(Wiggle fingers down as if raindrops.)
Comes the gentle rain.
And the five pretty sunflowers,
Lift their heads again.
(Hold five fingers up.)

The Pretty Flower

This is a flower.
(Cup hands.)
Open it wide.
(Open hands slowly.)
To show how pretty,
(Show "flower.")
It's made inside.

Activities

Pretty Pictures

Read *The Garden* by I. Sanchez and C. Peris or *Planting a Rainbow* by Lois Ehlert. Have the children decorate a Styrofoam drinking cup as a planter. Use markers, crayons, glue, material scraps, ribbon, etc.

Plant Seeds

Read *This Year's Garden* by Cynthia Rylant and *Growing Vegetable Soup* by Lois Ehlert. Then have the children plant seeds in their planters.

Supplies needed:

* planter
* potting soil
* seeds
* newspapers to cover the work area
* water
* plastic wrap
* rubber bands
* small pebbles *(optional, see note)*

Directions:

1. Add potting soil so the planter is about ⅛ full. Add the seeds and top with potting soil. (Be sure to check the seed package

directions as to the depth the seeds should be planted.)

2. Water the soil slightly and place a piece of plastic wrap over the cup with a rubber band. This will protect the cup on the way home.

Note: You will need to have the children place small pebbles in the bottom of the cup before adding the soil, or send a note home explaining that the planter will need a hole punched in the bottom and a jar lid placed underneath. This will allow the water to drain.

Fruit, Vegetable and Flower Art

Read *Seeds* by George Shannon or *The Rose in My Garden* by Arnold Lobel. Then have the children use fruits, vegetables and flowers to paint or stamp onto paper.

Supplies needed:

- fruit, vegetables or silk or plastic flowers
- paint
- cornstarch *(optional)*
- paper

Directions:

1. If you are using real fruits and vegetables cut them in various ways so that the same fruit or vegetable can paint or stamp differently.

2. Add cornstarch to the paint so it dries faster.

3. Have the children use the fruits, vegetables and flowers to paint a picture.

Gross Motor Skills Activity

Read *June 29, 1999* by David Wiesner or *Alison's Zinnia* by Anita Lobel.

Place silk flowers in planters around the room. If possible, have flowers that begin with your children's names available. Turn to a page in the book and ask the children to name the letter of the flower you name. Anyone whose name begins with that letter should go find the flower and stand next to it.

Seed Activities

- Bring in seed packets and have the children match the seeds to the vegetables.

- Cut different types of fruits in half to reveal the seeds. Have the children count how many seeds are in each half. Show that if one half has three seeds and the other half has two seeds the whole piece of fruit has five seeds. Will each piece of the same kind of fruit have the same amount of seeds?

- Bring in seeds that have been planted to show the various stages of growth. If you do not have a "green thumb" ask someone from your local nursery to come in for the day.

- Ask the children which kinds of seeds grow above the ground and which kind grow below the ground. You may want to use pictures in books to help reinforce the positional concept. Ask, "What do seeds need to grow?" Explain that just like us, they need sun and water (but not too much!).

- Place a full celery stalk in a glass of water that has food coloring in it. Talk about how plants drink water like we drink through a straw. Ask the children if they can predict what will happen when the celery drinks all of the water. Remind them to come look at the celery the next time they are in. Place it in an area where everyone can watch the results of the experiment. You can also place bean or sprout seeds between two wet paper towels and set them in the sunlight to sprout.

If you plan to plant your seedlings, give them to a day care, senior center or homeless shelter in your area. If you keep them, take pictures so that the progress can be recorded. If you have a bountiful harvest, ask the children who attended the program back for a feast of their efforts.

Fine Motor Skills Activity

Have various seeds out for the children to sort. Styrofoam trays and egg cartons work well for sorting. Use various colored trays for each seed sorted. Once the seeds are sorted ask the children to predict which group of seeds has the most, then count and verify.

Storytime Books to Share

Fiction Titles

Alison's Zinnia by Anita Lobel. William Morrow & Co., 1996. Alison acquired an amaryllis for Beryl who bought a begonia for Crystal and so on through the alphabet.

Anna's Garden Songs by Mary Q. Steele. Greenwillow Books, 1989. A collection of fourteen poems about the beet, potato, radish, onion and other plants found in the garden.

The Carrot Seed by Ruth Krauss. HarperCollins, 1989. A carrot seed planted by a little boy grows even though no one in his family believed it would.

City Green by DyAnne DiSalvo-Ryan. Morrow Junior Books, 1994. Marcy and Miss Rosa start a campaign to clean up an empty lot and turn it into a community garden.

Dancing in the Breeze by George Shannon. Bradbury Press, 1991. Lyrically describes Papa, young daughter and the evening breeze as they dance among the flowers in the front yard while the moon rises.

Flower Garden by Eve Bunting. Harcourt, 2000. Helped by her father, a young girl prepares a flower garden as a birthday surprise for her mother.

A Garden for Miss Mouse by Michaela Muntean. Parents Magazine Press, 1982. Miss Mouse plants a garden, which soon becomes more than she can handle.

The Gardener by Sarah Stewart. Farrar, Straus and Giroux, 2000. After her father loses his job, Lydia Grace goes to live with her Uncle Jim in the city, but takes her love for gardening with her.

The Garden of Happiness by Erika Tamar. Harcourt, 1996. Marisol and her neighbors turn a vacant New York City lot into a lush community garden.

The Gigantic Turnip by Alexei Tolstoy. Barefoot Books, 1999. A hilarious retelling of the classic Russian tale about a farmer whose turnip is impossible to pull out of the ground.

Growing Vegetable Soup by Lois Ehlert. Harcourt, 1990. A father and child grow vegetables and then make them into a soup.

Hands by Lois Ehlert. Harcourt, 1997. Detailed collages and unique, die-cut pages, enhance the charming story of a child's inspiration to build, paint and sew her own garden as she watches her parents work with their hands.

Home Lovely by Lynne Rae Perkins. Greenwillow Books, 1995. Hoping for trees or a flower garden, Tiffany transplants and cares for some seedlings that she finds and is surprised by what they become.

Jack's Garden by Henry Cole. William Morrow & Co., 1997. Cumulative text and illustrations depict what happens in Jack's garden after he plants his seeds.

June 29, 1999 by David Wiesner. Houghton Mifflin, 1995. While her third-grade classmates are sprouting seeds in paper cups, Holly has a more ambitious, innovative science project in mind.

The Lima Bean Monster by Dan Yaccarino. Walker & Co., 2001. After Sammy dumps the lima beans he does not want to eat, he starts a neighborhood trend to put rejected vegetables in a hole in a vacant lot, but a terrible lima bean monster rises to terrorize the town.

Paddington Bear in the Garden by Michael Bond. HarperCollins, 2002. Paddington sets out to create the most interesting garden he can.

Planting a Rainbow by Lois Ehlert. Harcourt, 1992. A mother and child plant a rainbow of flowers in the family garden.

The Poppy Seeds by Clyde R. Bulla. Penguin USA, 1994. A young boy's attempt to grow poppies in his drought-parched village softens the heart of the grouchy old man who has the village's only spring in his backyard.

The Rose in My Garden by Arnold Lobel. William Morrow & Co., 1993. A variety of flowers grow near the hollyhocks that give shade to the bee that sleeps on the only rose in a garden.

Seeds by George Shannon. Houghton Mifflin, 1994. When Warren moves away he misses his older friend next door and the times they shared in the garden, but the separation inspires each of them to do something creative about it.

This Year's Garden by Cynthia Rylant. Simon & Schuster, 1986. Follows the seasons of the year as reflected in the growth, life and death of the garden of a large rural family.

Tops and Bottoms adapted by Janet Stevens. Harcourt, 1995. By outwitting Lazy Bear, Hare manages to feed his hungry family.

Vegetable Garden by Douglas Florian. Harcourt, 1996. A family plants a vegetable garden and helps it grow to a rich harvest.

Nonfiction Books

Container Gardening for Kids by Ellen Talmage. Sterling Publishing, 1996. Provides instructions for propagating and caring for plants, with more than 20 beginning gardening projects.

The Garden by I. Sanchez and C. Peris. Barron's Educational Series, 1991. Explains about plant seeds, bulbs and flowers. Part of the Discovering Nature series.

Get Growing!: Exciting Indoor Plant Projects for Kids by Lois Walker. John Wiley & Sons, Inc., 1991. Presents 11 indoor gardening projects involving carrots, beans, potatoes, apples and other plants, and related cooking and handicraft activities.

Grow It For Fun by Denny Robson. Franklin Watts, 1991. An introduction to gardening with simple activities, such as growing beans and mushrooms, to more complicated projects, including a miniature garden in a bowl.

How a Seed Grows by Helene J. Jordan. HarperCollins, 1992. Uses observations of bean seeds planted in eggshells to demonstrate the growth of seeds into plants.

Let's Grow a Garden: A Step-by-Step Guide by Angela Wilkes. Dorling Kindersley Pub., 1997. A wonderfully illustrated step-by-step guide to planting and growing basics, including wildlife gardening, desert gardening and bottle gardens.

Little Green Thumbs by Mary An Van Hage. Millbrook Press, 1996. Provides ideas and instructions for projects that involve growing various kinds of plants indoors during the different seasons.

Tiny Green Thumbs by C. Z. Guest. Hyperion Books for Children, 2000. Tiny Bun and his grandmother plan, plant and grow a vegetable garden. Includes step-by-step instructions for planting carrots, beans, cucumbers, corn and sunflowers.

Other Media to Share

Magic School Bus Goes to Seed. Kid Vision/Scholastic (video) 1995. 30 minutes. Plants are featured in this Magic School Bus adventure.

Name Tag Patterns for Growing Great Books

Flying High Stories
Wind, Kites, Birds, Bats and Owls

Before Storytime

Name Tags

Copy the name tag patterns on page 97. Make enough copies so you have one name-tag per child. Cut the name tags out and color them if you like. Pin the name tag to the child's shirt or punch a hole in it and string it with yarn for a necklace.

Props

- ask a local pet shop or person in the community to bring in a pet bird

- nest hat (Turn a Styrofoam bowl and a Styrofoam dinner plate upside down. Glue the bowl to the plate. Punch holes on each side of the plate and string yarn through one hole, over the top of the bowl and through the other hole, leaving enough yarn so you can tie it under your chin. Cover the hat with tissue paper. Decorate with birds or raffia so it looks like a nest.)

- bat, owl and bird puppets

Storytime

- Introduce the theme by asking the children about their name tags.

- Ask, "Have you ever flown a kite?" "Have you ever seen an owl or a bat outside or in a zoo?" "Do you have a bird feeder or bath in your yard?"

- Sing the storytime song on page 7.

- Intersperse stories, fingerplays, songs and activities that fit your theme and time frame.

Snack

Serve "bird food mix." Mix together soy nuts (the roasted and salted kind are very good), sunflower seeds and pumpkin seeds.

Discussion Questions

Ask specific questions to reinforce comprehension concepts.

For example:

- "Do you remember how Bonnie Bumble got the baa back on the lamb in the story *One Windy Wednesday*?"

Wrapping It Up

Sing the goodbye song on page 8.

Songs

The Wind

Sung to the tune: "Skip To My Lou"

The wind is full of tricks today.
It almost blew me far away.
It almost blew me off my feet.
As I went walking down the street!

The next time that I go outside,
The wind won't take me for a ride.
Cause I know just what I will do—
I'll put some glue on the bottom of my shoe!

Blow, Blow, Blow the Wind

Sung to the tune: "Row, Row, Row, Your Boat"

Blow, blow, blow the wind,
Gently through the trees.
Blow and blow and blow and blow.
How I like a breeze!

Blow, blow, blow the clouds,
Blow them through the sky.
Blow and blow and blow and blow.
Watch the clouds roll by!

I See the Wind

Sung to the tune: "Hush Little Baby"

I see the wind when the leaves dance by.
(Dance hands around.)
I see the wind when the clothes wave "Hi!"
(Wave hand.)
I see the wind when the trees bend low.
(Bend arms over and down.)
I see the wind when the flags all blow.
(Wave arms high.)

I see the wind when the kites fly high.
(Raise arms high.)
I see the wind when the clouds float by.
(Wave hand gently.)
I see the wind when it blows my hair.
(Lift hair with hands.)
I see the wind most everywhere!
(Hold hands out, palms up.)

The Wind

Sung to the tune: "Here We Go Looby Loo"

Here we go up, up, up.
Here we go down, down, down.
Here we go forward.
Here we go backward.
Now we go round and round.

Noisy Wind

Sung to the tune: "The Farmer in the Dell"

I like the noisy wind,
I like the noisy wind.
It roars and mutters,
(Voice loud then soft.)
And it shakes the shutters.
(Shake hand tambourine style.)
I like the noisy wind.

I like the noisy wind,
I like the noisy wind.
It flaps the flag,

(Flap your arms back and forth.)
And rustles my bag.
(Rub hands together briskly.)
I like the noisy wind.

The Owl

Sung to the tune: "Head, Shoulders, Knees, and Toes"

Big eyes,
(Make two circles with fingers over eyes.)
Beaks and,
(Cup tips of fingers on one hand over nose and mouth to form a beak.)
Wings and claws,
(Flap arms once—freeze arm and bend fingers to look like a claw.)
Wings and claws.

Repeat

Who flies at night,
And says "Hoot! Hoot!"?
Big eyes,
Beaks and,
Wings and claws,
Wings and claws.

Fingerplays

I Saw a Little Bird

I saw a little bird,
(Place one finger pointing down on open palm.)
Go hop, hop, hop.
(Hop finger on palm.)
I told the little bird,
To stop, stop, stop.
(Hold up hand palm out.)

I went to the window,
(Cup both hands by eyes as if looking through a window.)
To say "How do you do?"
But he shook his little tail,
(Wiggle wrist back and forth with fingers outstretched and limp.)
And away he flew.
(Cross thumbs over each other and flap fingers as if to fly off like a bird.)

Five Little Blue Birds

Five little blue birds, hopping by my door,
One went away and now there are four.

Four little blue birds singing lustily,
One got away and now there are three.

Three little blue birds, and what should one do?
But go in search of dinner, leaving only two.

Two little blue birds singing for fun,
One flew away, and then there was one.

One little blue bird sitting in the sun,
He took a little nap, and then there was none.

Here is a Baby Bird

Here is a baby bird.
(Flap wings slowly and awkwardly.)
He is learning to fly.
(Flap wings faster.)
Now watch him get ready,
(Up on tiptoes.)
To take off to the sky.
(Jump softly.)

Five Little Robins

Five little robins lived in a tree.
(Hold up hand to show five fingers.)
Father, *(Thumb.)*
Mother, *(Thumb and index finger.)*
And baby makes three.
(Hold up three fingers.)

Father caught a worm.
(Make a catching motion.)
Mother caught a bug.
(Make a catching motion.)
The three little robins began to tug.
(Make tugging motion.)

This one got a bug,
(Hold up first finger.)
This one got a worm,
(Hold up second finger.)
This one said, "Now it's my turn."
(Hold up third finger.)

Four Little Birdies

Four little birdies high in the tree,
(Hold up four fingers.)
One flew away and now there are three.
(Fly one finger behind back, hold up three fingers.)

Three little birdies with feathers so new,
(Hold up three fingers.)
One flew away and now there are two.
(Fly one finger behind back, hold up two fingers.)

Two little birdies out in the sun,
(Hold up two fingers.)
One flew away and now there is one.
(Fly one finger behind back, hold up one finger.)

One little birdie alone in the nest,
(Hold up one finger.)
Afraid to fly out and join the rest.

Come little birdie, come fly like me.
(Wave hand toward you, flap arms, point to self.)
Come little birdie, fly out of the tree.
(Wave hand as to call to you, flap arms.)

Flap your wings, flap your wings down,
(Flap arms.)
So you can fly over a field and town.
(Flap arms.)
Up, up and away the birdie did fly,
(Hook thumbs together and flap fingers.)
Up and over the trees, up into the sky.
(Raise hands upward.)

Four little birdies now up so high,
(Raise four fingers in the air.)
I almost forgot to wave them "goodbye!"
(Wave goodbye.)

Bird Sounds

Big-eyed owl looks all around.
(Circle eyes with fingers, turn head left and right.)
Tiny sparrows sit on the ground.
(Squat down low.)
Ducks wiggle-waggle as they walk.
(Walk like a duck.)
Chickens scratch the ground and squawk.
(Slide feet, walk like a chicken.)
Ostriches are very tall.
(Reach hands high above head.)

Hummingbirds are very small.
(Hold index finger and thumb close together.)
"Peep, squawk, cheep and whoo" you heard,
(Move hands like beak while making the sounds.)
All of those are sounds of birds.

Owls

Owls in the treetop,
(Point upward.)
Proud and wise.
(Stick out chest, point to head.)
Here are his wings,
(Spread arms.)
And here are his eyes.
(Encircle eyes with fingers.)

Down on the ground,
(Point to ground.)
A mouse he spies,
(Wiggle fingers pointed toward the ground.)
Up he jumps, and off he flies!
(Spring up on toes and flap arms.)

Brown Owl

(Do appropriate actions. Clap hands as each numeral is said.)

Brown owl, brown owl,
Way up high in your tree,
Flap your feathery wings,
Just for me, 1, 2, 3.

Brown owl, brown owl,
Way up high in your tree,
Blink your golden eyes,
Just for me, 1, 2, 3.

Brown owl, brown owl,
Way up high in your tree,
Open your pointy beak,
Just for me, 1, 2, 3.

Brown owl, brown owl,
Way up high in your tree,
Sing an owl song,
Just for me, 1, 2, 3. (Hoot softly.)

Activities

Wind Paintings

Read *Lucky Song* by Vera B. Williams, *The Kite* by Mary Packard, *Kites* by Betinna Ling or *One Windy Wednesday* by Phyllis Root.

Supplies needed:

- newspaper
- paint smocks or old shirts
- box lid
- paper
- paint
- plastic spoon
- dish soap
- straw

Directions:

1. Cover your work surface with newspaper. Have the children wear paint smocks or old shirts.

2. Place a piece of paper in the box lid.

3. Add a drop of dish soap and water to the paint. Spoon a small amount of thinned paint onto the paper.

4. Have the children use a straw to blow the paint into various designs. When they use different colors, talk about how red and blue can make purple, etc.

Cat, Cat, Bird (Gross Motor Skills)

Read *The Best Nest* by P. D. Eastman or *Feathers for Lunch* by Lois Ehlert.

Have the children sit in a circle. One child is the "bird" first. He or she flaps his or her wings and encircles the seated children. The bird says "bird" or "cat" next to each child he or she walks behind. Once a seated child is called a "cat," he or she gets up and tries to catch the bird (explain that cats usually slink slowly toward birds, they do not run because that can scare away the bird) by tapping the bird's shoulder. The bird tries to get to safety by circling the group and sitting where the cat was seated. Once the bird succeeds, the cat becomes the new bird.

Bats and Owls

Read *Owly* by Mike Thaler, *Owl Babies* by Martin Waddell or *Stellaluna* by Janell Cannon. If you like, pass out bat rings (see Additional Storytime Resources on page 9).

Supplies needed:

- black or brown construction paper
- scissors
- white or black crayon
- glue

Directions:

1. Use the patterns on page 95 to make bats or owls. Copy the pattern pieces on black or brown paper.

2. Have the children cut out the wings and fold along the fold line.

3. Have them cut out the body pattern and draw on a face. A white crayon works best for the black paper and a black crayon for the brown paper.

4. If you are making bats, the children might want to add a mouth with fang teeth. For an owl, cut out a beak, fold it and glue it on.

5. Glue the wings to the sides of the body.

Science Activity

Show the children an egg and ask what they think will happen if you squeeze it. Discuss how this is an egg we eat, but that baby birds also hatch from eggs. Tell them about the various sizes and colors eggs can be depending on the bird. Hold an uncooked egg (make sure it has no cracks) in your hand. (You might want to do this over a pan, sink or dish, just in case!) Place the egg in the palm of your hand and squeeze. It should not break because you are putting pressure over the entire egg (when we crack an egg we strike it hard in one area). Because of the egg's design it can withstand pressure over the entire sur-

face. Nature designed it this way to protect it from animals that might want to harm the baby bird inside.

Fine Motor Skills Activity

Have the children count and sort various colors of feathers.

Gross Motor Skills Activity

Have the children pretend to be trees. Remind them that their feet are the roots of the trees. These are always planted firmly in the ground. Ask them to move the rest of their body as if the wind is blowing. Talk about how the wind blows hard or soft and how a tree looks during different seasons— full of leaves in the summer and bare in the winter. How might the children show these stages? What happens to the trees in the spring? What happens in the fall? As they move to the blowing wind, have them make the sound that a strong wind and a calm wind make. Strong winds can even make a tree bend all the way to the ground.

Kites

Supplies needed:

- craft sticks (seven for each kite frame)
- glue
- white tissue paper
- scissors
- markers
- streamers
- yarn *(optional)*

Directions:

1. Glue two craft sticks on top of each other.

2. Place one craft stick crosswise on top of the two vertical sticks.

3. Use four more sticks to create a diamond shape. Glue them to the kite frame.

4. Fold a full sheet of white tissue paper in half horizontally. Cut it into fourths. (A folded sheet is recommended for strength.)

5. Have the children decorate a section of the tissue paper with markers. Add glue on one side of the frame and place the decorated side of the tissue paper up. Place a dot of glue between the sheets of tissue to hold them together.

6. Turn the kite frame over and have the children trim off the excess tissue paper from the edge of the frame.

7. Add a streamer. If you like, tie small pieces of yarn to the tail.

Note: For younger children, or to lessen the time of this project, you might prepare the kite frames prior to your program.

Feather Painting

Supplies needed:

- smocks or old paint shirts
- paint
- paper
- feathers

Directions:

1. Have the children paint with feathers. You may wish to coordinate the color of the feathers to the color of the paint.

2. Have additional feathers available if the children wish to swirl or mix the paint colors on their paper.

Note: Add a small amount of dish soap to the paint for easier clean up.

Storytime Books to Share

Books About the Wind

Gilberto and the Wind by Marie Hall Ets. Penguin Putnam, 1978. A young boy discovers the wind is a playmate of many moods: one that can sail boats, fly kites, blow dirt and turn umbrellas inside out.

How Does the Wind Blow? by Lawrence F. Lowery. Holt, Rinehart & Winston, 1969. Describes the different things wind can do as a light breeze, strong wind or tornado.

How the Wind Plays by Michael Lipson. Hyperion Books, 1994. The wind, in the form of a mischie- vous child, indulges in such playful antics as shaking tree branches against windows and blowing snow inside.

One Windy Wednesday by Phyllis Root. Candlewick Press, 1996. The wind blows so hard that it blows the quack right out of the duck, the oink out of the pig and so on. Bonnie Bumble works hard to get each animal's sound back where it belongs.

While You Were Chasing a Hat by Lilian Moore. Harper Festival, 2001. While a little girl and her grandfather pursue her wayward hat, the wind fills the sails of boats, tugs at a kite, bends trees and more.

Books About Kites

Curious George Flies a Kite by H. A. Rey. Houghton Mifflin, 1958. A little monkey needs to be rescued when he tries to fly a kite.

The Kite by Mary Packard. Grolier, 1989. A child watches his kite fly high in the sky.

Kites by Betinna Ling. Scholastic, 1994. Simple language and illustrations show various shaped kites in a rainbow of colors.

Lucky Song by Vera B. Williams. Greenwillow Books, 1997. The song a little girl hears describes her kite-flying adventure.

Rabbit's Birthday Kite by Maryann Macdonald. Gareth Stevens Pub., 1999. After receiving a birthday kite from Hedgehog, impatient Rabbit learns that kite flying requires a few lessons.

Books About Bats

Bat in the Boot by Annie Cannon. Orchard Books, 1996. A family finds a baby bat in their mudroom and takes care of him until his mother comes back for him.

Bat Magic For Kids by Kathryn T. Lundberg. Gareth Stevens Pub., 1996. Relates information about the life, habits and natural history of bats.

Stellaluna by Janell Cannon. Harcourt, 1993. After Stellaluna accidentally lands in a bird's nest, the birds raise the baby fruit bat as one of their own. When she is finally reunited with her mother, she appreciates her differences and her new friendships.

Books About Owls

The Barn Owls by Tony Johnston. Charlesbridge Publishing, 2000. For at least 100 years, generations of barn owls have slept, hunted, called and raised their young and glided silently above the wheat fields around an old barn.

Good-Night Owl! by Pat Hutchins. Simon & Schuster, 1990. Because all of the other animals' noises keep him from sleeping, Owl watches for a chance to take his revenge.

I'm Only Afraid of the Dark (at Night!!) by Patti Stren. HarperCollins, 1982. Harold the owl's friend Gert schemes to help him get over his fear of the dark before the long dark winter begins.

Owl Babies by Martin Waddell. Candlewick Press, 1996. A comforting story about three baby owls that awake to find their mother gone. Huddled together and frightened, they await her return. Her arrival back home offers reassurance to youngsters who may share the young owls' fears.

Owl Moon by Jane Yolen. Putnam, 1987. On a winter's night under a full moon, a father and daughter trek into the woods to see the Great Horned Owl.

Owls by Elin Kelsey. Grolier, 1985. Facts and photographs of various kinds of owls. Part of the Nature's Children series.

Owly by Mike Thaler. Walker & Co., 1998. When Owly asks his mother question after question about the world, she finds just the right ways to help him find the answers.

Books About Birds

Are You My Mother? by P. D. Eastman. Random House, 1998. A little lost bird searches for its mother.

The Best Nest by P. D. Eastman. Random House, 1976. Mr. and Mrs. Bird look for a new home in a shoe, a mailbox and a church bell.

Birds by Ernestine Giesecke. Heinemann Library, 1998. Presents a brief introduction to the physical characteristics of birds and provides photographs and simple information to help the reader identify such birds as sparrows, finches, crows, ducks and hawks. Part of the Outside My Window series.

Feathers For Lunch by Lois Ehlert. Harcourt, 1996. An escaped house cat encounters twelve birds in the back yard, but fails to catch any of them and has to eat feathers for lunch.

Little Bird by Saviour Pirotta. American Natural Hygiene Society, 1992. Several animals suggest activities for a little bird who asks, "What can I do today?"

The Mountain That Loved a Bird by Alice McLerran. Aladdin Books, 2000. A beautiful bird brings life to a lonely, barren mountain.

This is the Bird by George Shannon. Houghton Mifflin, 1997. A cumulative tale about a wooden bird carved by a little girl's maternal ancestor and passed down lovingly from mother to daughter through the generations.

Patterns for Bats and Owls

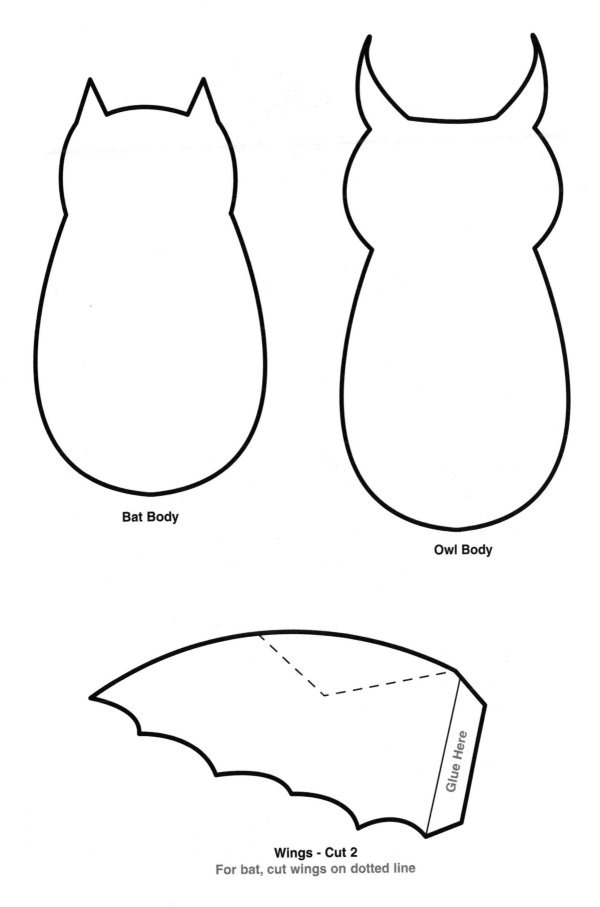

Bat Body

Owl Body

Glue Here

Wings - Cut 2
For bat, cut wings on dotted line

Name Tag Patterns for Flying High Stories

Name Tag Patterns for Flying High Stories

Stories Around Town

Community Workers and
People in the Neighborhood

Before Storytime

Name Tags

Copy the name tag patterns on page 104. Make enough copies so you have one name tag per child. Cut the name tags out and color them if you like. Pin the name tag to the child's shirt or punch a hole in it and string it with yarn for a necklace.

Props

- paintbrush, tape measure, wrench, play medical kit or real stethoscope, toothbrush and toothpaste, whisk, wooden spoon, comb, canvas bag (for mail carrier's pouch)

- If you enjoy costumes, dress in layers so that as your stories progress you are already wearing your outfit. Start with your street clothes (you will end up being your profession) and wear a light blue work shirt over your clothes. Apply a sticker over the breast pocket that says "mail carrier" and put USPS on your shoulder. Next layer an apron on top of your shirt. After that comes a lab coat, then cover all the costumes with work coveralls. With any of these costume suggestions you can always check a resale shop for inexpensive items as well as asking friends, neighbors or people in your community.

Storytime

- Introduce the theme by asking the children about their name tags.

- Ask, "Do you know who in your neighborhood would wear something like this?" Explain the word community and that it means people who live where we do and people who work and do jobs to help others that live nearby.

- Sing the storytime song on page 7.

- Intersperse stories, fingerplays, songs and activities that fit your theme and time frame.

Snacks

- Get rolls, doughnuts or muffins from the local bakery (you might ask if they will donate the snack).

- Serve a "tool mix" of pretzel twists (screws), licorice twist pieces (drill bits), thin pretzel sticks (nails), peanuts (nuts), circular gummy rings (washers) and raisins (nail plug caps).

- Make "paint brush cookies" ahead of time or with the children. Use any sugar cookie recipe or refrigerated cookie dough. Blend one egg yolk and ¼ teaspoon water. Divide mixture into separate cups for different colors. Add food coloring. Paint the designs on the cookies using small paintbrushes. If the paint thickens on standing, add a few drops of water. Bake the cookies as directed.

Discussion Questions

Ask specific questions to reinforce comprehension concepts.

Wrapping It Up

Sing the goodbye song on page 8.

Songs

I'm a Painter

Sung to the tune: "Frére Jacques"
Do as an echo song.

I'm a painter. *(Point to self.)*
I'm a painter. *(Point to self.)*
With a brush. *(Show brush.)*
With a brush. *(Show brush.)*
Dip it in the paint can. *(Dip brush in can.)*
Dip it in the paint can. *(Dip brush in can.)*
Not too much. *(Wiggle finger.)*
Not too much. *(Wiggle finger.)*

Brush goes upward. *(Brush up.)*
Brush goes upward. *(Brush up.)*
Brush goes down. *(Brush down.)*
Brush goes down. *(Brush down.)*
Now we use a roller. *(Pretend to roll on paint.)*
Now we use a roller. *(Pretend to roll on paint.)*
All around!
All around!

Who Am I?

Sung to the tune: "Oh When the Saints"

I am someone,
Who works with wood.
I use a hammer and some nails.
Sometimes I need screws and a drill
To make things we all use.

Benches and stairs,
Cabinets and chairs,
Dressers, desks and even beds.
Oh I can make things out of wood.
Who am I in your neighborhood?
(A carpenter)

A Mechanic

Sung to the tune: "Old MacDonald"

A mechanic fixes cars.
E-I-E-I-O
He oils this and tightens that.
E-I-E-I-O

With a pound, pound, here,
And a pound, pound there.
Here a pound, there a pound,
Everywhere a pound, pound.

A mechanic fixed my car,
Now I'll drive away!
BRRRRROOOOOOMMMM!

Doctors Make Us Well

Sung to the tune of "Farmer in the Dell"

The doctor makes us well.
The doctor makes us well.
Hey! Ho! What do you know?
The doctor makes us well.

My Doctor

Sung to the tune: "My Bonnie Lies Over the Ocean"

My doctor helps me when I feel bad.
She makes people feel well.
I really do like my doctor,
She helps everyone feel swell.

Doctors, doctors,
They help us feel much better,
Doctors, doctors,
They help us all when we're sick.

Brushing My Teeth

Sung to the tune: "London Bridges"

Here's my toothpaste,
Here's my brush,
I won't hurry,
I won't rush.
Working hard to keep teeth clean,
Front and back and in between.

So I brush and brush and brush and brush.
I won't hurry,

I won't rush.
When I brush for quite a while,
I will have a happy smile.

My Dentist

Sung to the tune: "Frére Jacques"
Do as an echo song.

My dentist,
My dentist,
Always tells me,
Always tells me,
Brush your teeth,
Brush your teeth,
Twice a day.
Twice a day.

Always floss,
Always floss,
Every day.
Every day.
Keep your teeth healthy.
Keep your teeth healthy.
Your smile is great!
Your smile is great!

Firefighters

Sung to the tune: "Are You Sleeping?"

I'm a firefighter,
I'm a firefighter,
Watch me go!
Watch me go!
See how all the people shout,
When we put the fire out
With a hose.
With a hose.

Do You Know the Mailman?

Sung to the tune: "Muffin Man"

Do you know the mailman,
The mailman, the mailman?
Do you know the mailman,
Delivers letters to you?

They can be a boy or girl,
A boy or girl, a boy or girl.
They deliver letters,
And packages to you.

Fingerplays

The Chef

I really love to cook.
(Point to self.)
I am a cook you see.
I chop and cook and bake
Until around three.
(Pretend to chop, hold up three fingers.)

Mixing, pouring, rolling,
(Pretend to mix, pour and use a rolling pin.)
Soups, potatoes, rolls,
(Rub tummy.)
Veggies, fruits, meats and even doughnut
holes! *(Use two fingers to make a circle.)*

Working to make foods,
That are good for you and me.
(Point to children and self.)
Take a taste,
And you will see!
(Pretend to offer tasting spoon.)

I Want to Go

I want to go to the library,
And read all the books that I can see.
I want to read about teddy bears, ants and
bees.
I'll learn about noses, eyes and ears,
Plants and flowers, even trees.
I need a book about the spoon,
That ran away with the dish,
And one that teaches me how to fish.
I'd check out books—one, two, three,
If I was at the library.

Johnny Pounds *Traditional*

(A good book to read before this fingerplay is A
Carpenter by Douglas Florian.)

Johnny pounds with one hammer,
(Sit on floor with legs straight out in front.)
One hammer, one hammer.
(Pound one fist onto thigh lightly.)
Johnny pounds with one hammer,
Now he pounds with two.
(Pound two fists onto thighs.)

Johnny pounds with two hammers,
Two hammers, two hammers.
Johnny pounds with two hammers,
Now he pounds with three.
(Pound two fists onto thighs and bounce one leg.)

Johnny pounds with three hammers,
Three hammers, three hammers.
Johnny pounds with three hammers,
Now he pounds with four.
(Pound two fists and two legs.)

Johnny pounds with four hammers,
Four hammers, four hammers.
Johnny pounds with four hammers,
Now he pounds with five.
(Pound with two fists, two legs and nod head.)

Johnny pounds with five hammers,
Five hammers, five hammers.
Johnny pounds with five hammers,
Now he goes to sleep.
(Fold hands next to cheek, as if to sleep.)

Activities

Gross Motor Skills Activity

Read *Stop Those Painters!* by Rita Golden Gelman.

Have the children pretend to hold a paint can and paintbrush. They should pretend to paint fast, slow, up, down, however you call out until you say "stop those painters!" Repeat.

Cars and Trucks

Read *An Auto Mechanic* by Douglas Florian and *How Many Trucks Can a Tow Truck Tow?* by Charlotte Pomerantz.

Supplies needed:

- crayons or markers
- scissors
- glue
- light cardboard
- yarn
- milk caps
- bottle cork
- inkpad

Directions:

1. Copy the patterns on page 69, one tow truck and car for each child. Cut out the pieces and trim off the wheels.
2. Have the children color the truck and car.
3. Glue the pieces onto light cardboard and have the children decorate the background.
4. Add yarn for the tow chain and use milk caps for the tow truck's tires.
5. Use a bottle cork and inkpad to stamp the tires for the car.

Toothbrush Painting

Read *Freddie Visits the Doctor* by Nicola Smee, *Brush Your Teeth, Please* by Leslie McGuire, *Freddie Visits the Dentist* by Nicola Smee or *Mr. Cookie Baker* by Monica Wellington.

Supplies needed:

- toothbrushes
- paint
- paint smocks or old shirts
- paper

Directions:

1. Have the children wear smocks or old shirts to protect their clothing.
2. Add dish soap to the paint for easier clean up.
3. Have the children dip old toothbrushes in paint and run their fingers over the bristles to splatter the paint on the paper. They can also use the toothbrush as a paintbrush.

Note: *You might offer the children tooth-shaped paper for their painting.*

Gross Motor Skills Activity

Read *Who's Got Mail?* by Charles Reasoner, *Never Mail an Elephant* by Mike Thaler, *Library Lil* by Suzanne Williams or *Miss Bindergarten Takes a Field Trip With Kindergarten* by Joseph Slate.

Have the children sit in a circle. One child is the first "player." Whisper in the player's ear a community helper to act out. (For younger children, you might say "show how a firefighter would use the hose to put out a fire.") The other children in the circle try to guess what person the player is acting out.

Suggestions are: police, doctor, hairstylist or barber, driver (taxi, truck or bus), school crossing guard, waiter/waitress, etc.

Math Activity

Have different colored envelopes on a table for the children to count and sort, just as a mail carrier does when he or she delivers the mail. Save stamp-like stickers from junk mail offers to use as postage on the letters. Make a mailbox from a cardboard soda carton. Place the box flat and tape the bottom flap to the sides so it stays shut. The top flap will open and close as the mailbox door. Cover the box with paper and decorate as a mailbox. Attach a flag with a brass brad so that it can go up and down. This is also a good art project for the children to do.

Fine Motor Skills Activity

Have different sizes of nuts, washers, bolts and screws available for the children to put together. If possible, have a piece of scrap wood with holes drilled in it and a screwdriver so the children can use tools as a carpenter would.

Storytime Books to Share

The Adventures of Taxi Dog by Debra and Sal Barracca. Penguin Putnam, 2000. Maxi, a stray dog, is adopted by the driver of a Checker cab, who takes Maxi along on his daily rounds.

An Auto Mechanic by Douglas Florian. William Morrow & Co., 1994. Simple text and illustrations introduce the daily work of an automobile mechanic.

Barney & B. J. Go to the Police Station by Mark S. Bernthal. Lyrick Studios, 1998. Illustrated with photographs, Barney and B. J. show what a police officer does.

Brush Your Teeth, Please by Leslie McGuire. Reader's Children's Publishing, 1993. Learn about dental hygiene with a shark that flosses, a chimp that brushes back and forth and others.

Carla the Carpenter by Cathy East Dubowski. Penguin USA, 1992. Carla Beaver shows how a carpenter makes things from wood, even a house for giraffes.

A Carpenter by Douglas Florian. HarperCollins, 1991. A simple description of what a carpenter does in daily work.

Ernie the Electrician by Cathy East Dubowski. Penguin USA, 1992. Ernie Beaver helps out the townspeople by fixing all things that are electrical.

Dot the Firedog by Lisa Desimini. Scholastic, 2001. Dot the Dalmatian lives at a firehouse and accompanies the firefighters when they rush to a burning house.

Freddie Gets a Haircut by Nicola Smee. Little Barron's, 1999. Freddie goes to the hairdresser to get a haircut.

Freddie Visits the Dentist by Nicola Smee. Little Barron's, 2000. Freddie and his bear go for a dental checkup.

Freddie Visits the Doctor by Nicola Smee. Little Barron's, 1999. Freddie gets a sore throat and goes to see the doctor.

How Many Trucks Can a Tow Truck Tow? by Charlotte Pomerantz. Random House, 1997. One little tow truck rescues three tow trucks.

I Want to Be a Vet by Dan Liebman. Firefly Books, 2000. Simple text and photographs show the various jobs of a veterinarian.

Library Lil by Suzanne Williams. Penguin Putnam, 2001. A formidable librarian makes readers not only out of the once resistant residents of her small town, but out of a tough talking, television-watching, motorcycle gang as well.

Milo the Mechanic by Cathy East Dubowski. Penguin USA, 1992. Milo Beaver is a busy mechanic, his garage is always busy, he's so busy he even forgets his birthday!

Miss Bindergarten Takes a Field Trip With Kindergarten by Joseph Slate. Penguin Putnam, 2001. Miss Bindergarten and her kindergarten are stepping out in style to visit and explore exciting places around town.

Mr. Cookie Baker by Monica Wellington. Dutton, 1992. After a day of making and selling cookies, Mr. Baker gets to enjoy one himself.

Mr. Griggs' Work by Cynthia Rylant. Orchard Books, 1993. Mr. Griggs lives, breathes and adores his work at the post office.

My Dog is Lost! by Ezra Jack Keats. The Puffin Group, 1999. Two days after arriving in New York from Puerto Rico, eight-year-old Juanito, who speaks no English, loses his dog and searches all over the city for it making new friends along the way.

Never Mail an Elephant by Mike Thaler. Troll Associates, 1994. The narrator has trouble mailing an elephant as a birthday present to Cousin Edna.

Officer Buckle and Gloria by Peggy Rathmann. Putnam, 1995. The children at Napville Elementary School always ignore Officer Buckle's safety tips, until a police dog named Gloria accompanies him when he gives his safety speeches.

Policeman Small by Lois Lenski. Random House, 2001. Policeman Small gets to see a lot of what goes on in town. He's at his post, directing traffic, by six o'clock in the morning. On one busy day, Policeman Small makes sure the town's kids get to school safely. He also helps an ambulance and fire truck get through the intersection, and even leads a parade on his motorcycle. During the rush, Policeman Small spreads his cheer by saying hello to all the people passing in cars.

Stop That Garbage Truck! by Linda Glaser. A. Whitman, 1993. Shy Henry eagerly waits to see his "buddy" on the garbage truck every time it comes—and finally manages to speak on a day when there is a small emergency.

Stop Those Painters! by Rita Golden Gelman. Scholastic, 1989. Painters come and paint everywhere and everything; they must be stopped!

Uncle Jed's Barbershop by Margaree King Mitchell. Simon & Schuster, 1997. Despite serious obstacles and setbacks, Sarah Jean's Uncle Jed, the only black barber in the county, pursues his dream of saving enough money to open his own barbershop.

Where Does the Mail Go? A Book About the Postal System by Melvin and Gilda Berger. Ideals Publications, 2001. Shows how mail gets from place to place.

Who's Got Mail? by Charles Reasoner. Penguin Putnam, 2000. Lift the flaps, see through slots and see a surprise special delivery at the end.

Community Helpers Series

School Bus Drivers by Dee Ready. Capstone Press, 1998. Explains the dress, tools, training and work of school bus drivers as well as special features of their business.

School Crossing Guards by Terri DeGezelle. Capstone Press, 2001. A simple introduction to the work school crossing guards do, the tools they use and the clothing they wear as well as their importance to the community they serve.

Truck Drivers by Karen Bush Gibson. Capstone Press, 2000. Introduces the work truck drivers do, the kind of vehicles they drive, the training they need and the people who help them.

We Need Mail Carriers by Lola M. Schaefer. Capstone Press, 1999. Simple text and photographs describe mail carriers and their role in our communities.

In My Neighborhood Series

Fire Fighters by Paulette Bourgeois. Kids Can Press, 1998. Describes what firefighters do, how they dress and fire prevention tips.

Postal Workers by Paulette Bourgeois. Kids Can Press, 1998. Shows postal workers and what they do.

Name Tag Patterns for Stories Around Town

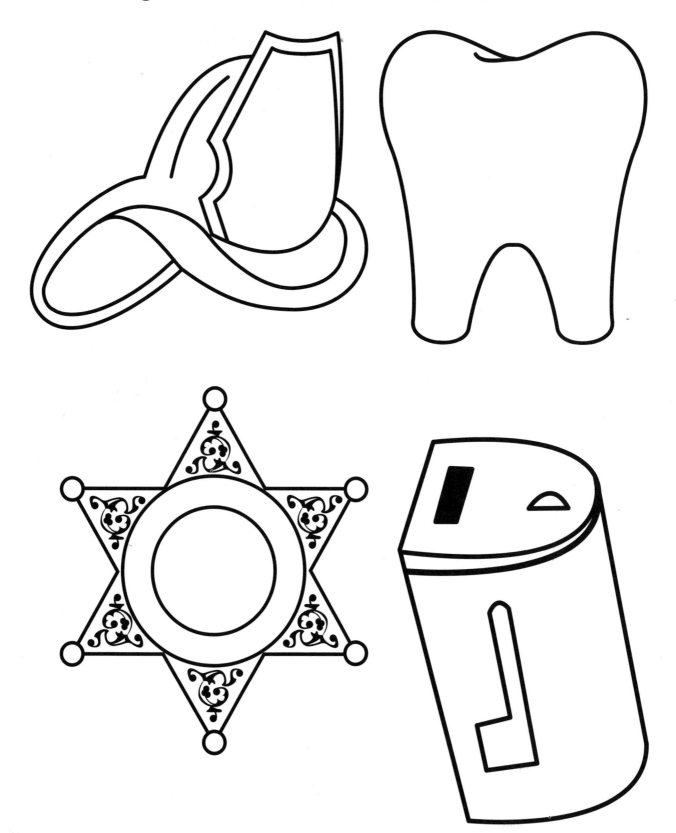